Death by Pastoring

Finding the Heartbeat of a Healthy Leader

Shane and Sue Schlesman

AVAIL

Copyright © 2024 by Shane and Sue Schlesman

Published by AVAIL

All rights reserved. No portion of this book may be reproduced, stored in a retrieval system, or transmitted in any form or by any means—electronic, mechanical, photocopy, recording, scanning, or other—except for brief quotations in critical reviews or articles, without prior written permission of the author.

Unless otherwise noted, scripture quotations are taken from the Holy Bible, New International Version®, NIV®. Copyright © 1973, 1978, 1984, 2011 by Biblica, Inc.™ Used by permission of Zondervan. All rights reserved worldwide. www.zondervan.com. The "NIV" and "New International Version" are trademarks registered in the United States Patent and Trademark Office by Biblica, Inc.™ | Scripture quotations marked KJV are taken from the King James Version of the Bible. Public domain. | Scripture quotations marked MSG are taken from THE MESSAGE, copyright © 1993, 1994, 1995, 1996, 2000, 2001, 2002 by Eugene H. Peterson. Used by permission of NavPress. All rights reserved. Represented by Tyndale House Publishers, Inc. | Scripture quotations marked NLT are taken from the Holy Bible, New Living Translation, copyright © 1996, 2004, 2015 by Tyndale House Foundation. Used by permission of Tyndale House Publishers, Inc., Carol Stream, Illinois 60188. All rights reserved. | Scripture quotations marked TLB are taken from The Living Bible copyright © 1971 by Tyndale House Foundation. Used by permission of Tyndale House Publishers Inc., Carol Stream, Illinois 60188. All rights reserved. The Living Bible, TLB, and The Living Bible logo are registered trademarks of Tyndale House Publishers.

For foreign and subsidiary rights, contact the author.

Cover design by Sara Young
Cover photo by Andrew van Tilborgh

ISBN: 978-1-960678-74-4   1 2 3 4 5 6 7 8 9 10

Printed in the United States of America

WHAT PEOPLE ARE SAYING ABOUT
Death by Pastoring

"Shane and Sue have addressed the elephant in the room: pastors don't know how to talk about their overwhelming stress or how to get healthy. *Death by Pastoring* addresses a critical topic for pastoral leadership—reorienting your personal life towards spiritual and physical health before it's too late. This book is a must-read for pastors, non-profit leaders, pastoral staffs, and ministry spouses. As the Church, we cannot wait any longer to get real about the impact of stress and anxiety on pastors and their leadership."

—*Mark Batterson, NYT Bestselling Author of* The Circle Maker *and Lead Pastor of National Community Church*

"I love it when an author speaks from experience, not just theory. In *Death by Pastoring*, Shane and Sue provide an outstanding playbook for pastors on living the assignment of their calling rather than getting burned out. You will discover the peace that comes from being yoked to Jesus and the calm that He brings when you lie down in His green pastures."

—*Doug Clay, General Superintendent of the Assemblies of God*

"Shane and Sue are the perfect discussion leaders for a critical conversation about pastor burn-out. I've had a front-row seat to the painful and purposeful changes Shane and Sue have made during a stressful leadership season. They have pursued freedom from anxiety, not an exodus from church or faith. *Death by Pastoring* is a must-read for every ministry leader."

—*Scott Wilson, Founder and President of Ready Set Grow and 415 Leaders*

"Stress and anxiety convince us that we are all alone and that no one understands the pressure we endure as pastors. Through personal stories, Biblical wisdom, and authenticity, Shane and Sue remind us that we are not alone, and that change is possible. If you are a pastor and are tired of feeling overwhelmed, this book will reconnect you with the Good Shepherd and help you walk with him to a place of renewal and hope."

—Justin Davis, Pastor, Co-founder of RefineUs Ministries and USA Today Bestselling Author of Being Real > Being Perfect: How Transparency Leads to Transformation

"Those who lead churches can find many fine books to hone their leadership skills. However, too few honestly look at the stress and hardships resulting from leading. Without integrating emotional health with our spiritual life and leadership, pastors fall away, quit, or die trying. *Death by Pastoring* gives us an honest look at hardships and provides practices to move toward health and wholeness. Shane and Sue lay out a paradigm shift to encourage and empower overwhelmed leaders."

—Frank Potter, District Superintendent of Assemblies of God Potomac Ministry Network, and Lisa Potter, Author of The Collective Journey *and Executive Director of Women Who Lead*

"Shane and Sue are the perfect examples of what it means to lead and suffer. They have walked through the stress of leading and transitioning a growing church. They will help many pastors lead ministries from a position of health."

—Travis Jones, Co-Pastor of Motivation Church and Church Planting Strategist for Church Multiplication Network

"Far too many pastors and their wives hover on the edge of weariness and burnout. Shane and Sue show us the way to lead and live well without losing the best of who we are. Rich in wisdom and steeped in authenticity, this is a must-read for anyone in ministry."

—Angela Donadio, Ministry Leader, Author, and Host of the Make Life Matter *Podcast*

"Pastoral ministry can be unrelenting and overwhelming, and the pressure it creates can produce unexpected outcomes. Leaning into their own stories of stress and its crushing effects on the mind, body, and spirit, Shane and Sue Schlesman provide profoundly Biblical and practical insights to help you chart a new path forward. *Death by Pastoring* offers more than a few tips to navigate stress. It's a powerful guide to create a life-giving rhythm for a hope-filled future."

—Stephen and Karen Blandino, LPC,
Authors and Pastors of 7 City Church

"I'm so thankful that Shane and Sue have brought this important conversation into the light. My family and I have been personally impacted by their ministry. As leaders, they prioritize the kingdom of God over the pressures of church ministry. All of us, as ministry leaders and Christ-followers, must receive God's call to restoration, especially during our painful seasons. This important book will help you reorient your soul to a kingdom that lasts forever."

—Tony Fitzgerald, Founder of Church of the Nations

"*Death By Pastoring* is a necessary resource for any leader looking to grow, heal, and lead with healthy boundaries. Sue and Shane give us all a glimpse into real-life ministry stressors from their personal experience; then they provide a map to recover with hope. This book is a breath of fresh air. It's sure to affirm and encourage every pastor."

—Brittany Jones, Co-Pastor of Motivation Church,
Mental Health Advocate, and Founder of KNOWN

"A must-read for pastors and their spouses. Shane and Sue address the core issues of pastoral stress and present solutions for the unique challenges of ministry. We strongly endorse this book as it brings sustainability and encouragement to your calling."

—Pastor Brad and Heidi Mitchell, Lead Pastors of The
River Church and Co-Founders of Build Your Marriage

"As a forty-two-year veteran leading churches, schools, and ministries, I have observed that ministerial health in America is in a precarious state. Leaders have endured catalytic moments of distress. Shane and Sue are exemplary leaders who pivoted during a painful season and emerged stronger and more effective in their mission. After Shane's stress-induced heart attack, my dear friends determined to become better, not bitter; these champions became heroes who command my admiration. Their message of hope has become a valuable blessing to leaders at their retreats, conferences, and staff consultations. I have personally benefitted from their keen insights. Since they have now packaged their principles in this book, thousands more will be empowered to mitigate their stress and become victors instead of victims."
—*Mark Morrow, Lead Pastor of CrossWalk Church*

"As pastors of a multi-site church, we are keenly aware of the dangers of mismanaged stress. We have personally watched Shane and Sue's journey from stress to rest, which came at a high cost. God's call for us as ministers of the gospel is not to work harder but to work healthier. This book is the clarion call needed for church leaders everywhere."
—*Kyle and Marcia Bethke, Lead Pastors of One Church*

"Stress tells us that a particular pressure exceeds our resources to deal with it. The stress upon every leader is unique, especially leaders in helping professions. All too often, a leader's self-care routine is missing from stress management. Shane and Sue have provided a resource for stressed-out pastors and leaders to move forward from a place of restoration and health. This book is a worthy addition to any self-care toolbox."
—*Jeremy Lanning, LPC, CCPT, CLC, CBC,*
Counselor and Psychotherapist

For the men and women who pastor faithfully, lead ministries, and live out the kingdom on the earth. Your labor is not in vain. We pray this book helps you serve, love, and grow from a place of peace and rest.

"Let us not become weary in doing good, for at the proper time we will reap a harvest if we do not give up."

—GALATIANS 6:9

ACKNOWLEDGMENTS

Writing a book is always a team effort.

Martijn, thank you for sitting with us while we shared our personal stress stories and passionately lamented the epidemic unhealthiness of church leaders across the country. You convinced us to put God's message of restful work into book form, and you provided the platform to do it. We appreciate you believing in our message.

Thank you, Amy, Debbie, Sarah, Allison, and the rest of the team at Four Rivers and AVAIL for your kind and careful attention to every detail of the publication process of *Death by Pastoring*. You were a dream to work with.

Sam Chand, we're grateful for your influence and encouragement. Thank you for listening, sharing your wisdom, and writing the foreword to this book. We love your ministry, and we're always grateful to learn from you.

Thank you to Scott Wilson, Mark Brewer, and the Ready, Set, Grow team—you are our brothers in the fight for double-kingdom impact. Thank you for walking with us and guiding us through some difficult waters.

Thank you to the *Stress Test* Podcast team, our guests, and tech engineers. You were grossly underpaid (or not paid)! But you made it possible for us to reach out to listeners with advice and support so all of us can lead more balanced spiritual, physical, emotional, and intellectual lives. Thank you to everyone who subscribes and listens to *Stress Test* Podcast. We hope you've been blessed by the content.

Bruce, Brent, Brady, Tracy, and Casey—we love you. We're so proud of you. We pray for you to enjoy lives of purpose and peace, to serve Jesus without internal or external stress and pressure, and to know that you truly belong to Him and to our family. We pray that you will work and rest better than we have. Your existence and love are the biggest blessings of our lives.

Thank you to Dave and Amy for a lifetime of friendship. Your personal support has been a lifeline to us emotionally and spiritually. With you, we are always ourselves. We're grateful for the years of crying, laughing, dreaming, and ministering together. Here's to many more.

To our church family and all our spiritual brothers and sisters who have supported, encouraged, and championed us throughout difficult years—thank you. We are so grateful. You are our personal friends, faithful co-laborers in ministry, ardent prayer partners, and committed spiritual mentors. You are too many in number to list here. We value your consistent friendship and support more than we could express in a paragraph. God has equipped you for many ministry assignments, but your standing as watchmen on the wall for us has been profoundly extraordinary and humbling.

To all the readers of *Death by Pastoring*, thank you for giving us the opportunity to be a part of your journey toward personal and pastoral health. We may not know you individually, but if you pastor people, we know you. We see you. Please believe that, because of Jesus, your best days are still ahead.

Most of all, we're grateful to our Lord Jesus Christ, who calls us into His ministry and equips us to serve when we choose to obey. We praise God for life, for salvation, and for the loving relationships He gives us. Praise to the Lord.

FOREWORD

Pastoring is the second hardest job.

A Pastor sees the wear and tear of life more than any other professional. A doctor sees you for physical needs. An attorney sees you for legal needs. A builder sees you for building needs. An insurance agent sees you for insurance needs. A banker sees you for financial needs.

A Pastor? A Pastor sees you for every need.

The Pastor sees families when babies are being born and when family members die. When people are getting married and when they're getting divorced. When people are employed gainfully as well as they are unemployed and struggling. When sons and daughters are serving the Lord and when they are bringing heartache to the family. Up and down. Joy and distress.

And it never stops. It is daily.

If pastoring is the second hardest job, what is the hardest? Being married to the Pastor.

Carrying second-hand disappointments, pains, setbacks, hurts, and callousness is harder than when it is directed at you. A Pastor's spouse usually doesn't have forums to discuss all that.

A Pastor can vent to their boards, staff persons, lay leaders, other Pastors, or their denominational leaders—venting may not be helpful, but at least Pastors have forums for discussion. None of those are usually available to the Pastor's spouse.

A Pastor's work is never finished. A Pastor never goes home saying "I am done with everything." Never. Ministry work is relentless. Working and living with no finish lines heavily taxes the spirit, mind, and body.

A Pastor will never be on a total vacation, ever. An electrician, a plumber, an attorney, a teacher, or a doctor can pass on responsibilities or even close shop to take a vacation. Most professionals can shut their phones and emails off. Not a Pastor. They're on mentally all the time; they cut their vacations short to return to the church for emergencies. The Pastor is always on.

There are unrealistic expectations placed on Pastors by themselves, the church, and denominational leaders. Professional baseball players who are paid millions a year do well if they get a hit a fraction of the time at bat; most often, big league hitters strike out at the plate. But a Pastor is expected to hit one out of the ballpark every time they get to bat. Every sermon. Every event. When addressing ministry expectations, I always tell Pastors, "You're only as good as last Sunday!" How unrealistic is that?

When a Pastor visits someone in the hospital or conducts a funeral, is that done routinely? No! These are people the Pastor loves and cares for, and a Pastor experiences a deep sense of loss to carry their burdens with them. The same Pastor who conducts the funeral of a beloved member on a Saturday is expected to hit a grand slam the next day. Who comforts the Pastor? Or is the Pastor viewed as a heartless automaton who's never affected by his people's trauma?

Isolation is the most common factor that methodically weakens the internal, spiritual, and relational immune system. It's hard for Pastors to have real friends. Finding friends in the church who can handle the complexities of a Pastor's life is rare. Pastors can't share everything—so much is confidential. Most Pastors who have real friends find them outside their church, often in other cities.

One of a Pastor's difficult pains occurs when people who were discipled, developed, and deployed in their church simply walk away. No conversation. No goodbye. No warning. Just missing in action. Most people leave church over petty items that conflict with their personal preferences. The Pastor fields questions about them. The Pastor mourns their loss. The Pastor is left with questions. Pastors discover that the people you help the most will be the first to leave. It's a revolving door that never stops.

My friends Shane and Sue Schlesman have poured their hearts into this book you hold in your hands. It is transparent and transformational. It offers understanding and wisdom. It encourages pragmatic steps that reverse death by pastoring so that one day, Pastors can experience life by pastoring.

Well done, Shane and Sue!

—Sam Chand
Author of *Leadership Pain*

CONTENTS

Acknowledgments ix
Foreword xiii

PART 1. The Silent Killer *(The Problem of Stress)* 19
   CHAPTER 1. The Almost-Death of A Pastor
                   (and His Wife) 21
   CHAPTER 2. The DNA of Stress 35
   CHAPTER 3. What We Didn't Learn in Seminary. 49
   CHAPTER 4. The Snare of Expectations 61
   CHAPTER 5. A Bottomless Pit 75

PART 2. A New Way to Work (The Hope for Stress) 89
   CHAPTER 6. A Message For the Heavy-Hearted 91
   CHAPTER 7. The Pathway to Peace 107
   CHAPTER 8. Leading in a Yoke 123
   CHAPTER 9. Stewards and Owners. 139
   CHAPTER 10. A Lighter Load 149

PART 3. A New Way to Rest (the Redemption Of Stress) . . 159
   CHAPTER 11. The Good Shepherd 161
   CHAPTER 12. Rest Versus Restoration. 171
   CHAPTER 13. New Walk, Same Valley 183

| CHAPTER 14. | A Seat at the Table | 199 |
| CHAPTER 15. | The House of the Lord | 213 |

Other Resources by Shane and Sue Schlesman 219

Resources 221

Sources 247

PART 1:

THE SILENT KILLER
(The Problem of Stress)

"Answer me, O LORD, out of the goodness of your love; in your great mercy turn to me. Do not hide your face from your servant; answer me quickly, for I am in trouble."

—Psalm 69:16-17

CHAPTER 1

THE ALMOST-DEATH OF A PASTOR
(and His Wife)

At mile thirty-six, while pulling my team up the final ascent, I (Shane) felt a stabbing pain in my chest. I pulled off the front to recover, drafting from the bikers flying past me. I tucked into the back of the Peloton, expecting to sit in their draft to lower my heart rate, which was pushing 195.

I couldn't recover or catch my breath, even on the descent. A harsh pain hammered my chest. A teammate slowed and asked me how I was.

"I'm good," I panted. *How could I be this out of shape?* I gave my teammate a weak thumbs-up to go on without me. My legs slowed in revolutions. I drifted away from the pack, pedaling lightly, panting, checking my numbers. Still 195. Not good.

Slowly, I pedaled alone back to my car and drove home. I stopped for gas on the way. At home, I showered painfully and told myself nothing was wrong.

Epic pastor-perspective: *Grit your teeth and pray. You'll get through it.*

When my wife Sue found me hunched over the kitchen counter, breathing heavily and unable to eat, she gave me two adult-strength aspirin and insisted I go to the hospital because I was having a heart attack.

I dismissed the crazy suggestion but lay down on the couch. My doctors had always raved about what great shape my body and heart were in. I was certainly not having a heart attack.

At that point, my son Brent, a physical therapist, walked into the house. He took my blood pressure. Normally 120/80, it was already at 160/100. Three separate times, Brent manually took my blood pressure. It kept climbing. Sue was already upstairs packing a bag. When my blood pressure hit 180/120, I agreed to go to the hospital.

The ER nurse took blood and hooked me up to two EKG machines, which both indicated a healthy heart. The doctor wasn't sure why my heart seemed distressed. Pain medication dripped through the IV. My heart rate and blood pressure slowed. The pain decreased. I felt tired but more like my post-race self.

"We're going to let you rest a bit before you go home. We don't think it's a heart attack," said the ER doctor.

A heart attack? How was this possible?

Then, a male nurse, only three months into nursing, studied my numbers and shook his head. "I know I'm not as experienced as everyone here," he said, "but something's wrong with these EKGs." He paused, uncomfortable. "You should listen to the doctor . . . but I think I'd want to call the cardiologist."

"Call him," we said.

Minutes later, the cardiologist entered my room. "I've checked your blood work. You've got cardiac enzymes in your blood. You've had a heart attack," he said. "I've called my team. They'll be here in 30 minutes. I'll do a heart catheterization first to see what the problem is."

A heart attack? How was this possible?

THE SILENT KILLER

Many mental health experts refer to stress as "the silent killer." We never think our stress is as dangerous as it actually is.

We all have stress. We're used to it. We complain about it. We even brag about it. We compare our stress to other people's. If we're endurance athletes, like I am, we experience stress as part of the training process. I max out my heart rate on purpose.

For years, I had endured long work hours, the weight of pastoral care, the abuse from angry members, the tiredness. At first, I thrived on it.

I acclimated to the insomnia, the panic attacks, the stomach aches, the muscle tension. I saw doctors, chiropractors, massage therapists, physical therapists, pharmacists. When my body craved change, I responded with grit and tenacity. I never slowed because my ministry never slowed.

Without realizing it, I engaged in silent, systematic, and intentional dying.

Physicians surmise that 80% of their patients' symptoms are stress-related. Cancer, stroke, body pain, digestion, insomnia, anxiety, depression, and other diseases are all linked to stress and its negative effects on the body. I'm guessing you handle stress like I did.

We all take vacations. We exercise. We change our diet and take some pills. We keep going, running at break-neck speed, trying to save the world. We're living for Jesus, after all. Our families understand. They're ministering right along with us. We're at church every day, and we love it. We're saving the world.

All the while, we're killing ourselves.

CUE THE WIFE

At 11 pm, while we waited for the cardiac team to arrive, I (Sue) called our kids—all young adults—to come to the hospital and see Shane before his heart catheterization. The cardiologist hadn't promised what he'd find. It could turn into open-heart surgery. It had been nearly six hours already since Shane's heart attack. We were already lucky.

"But Dad's an Ironman," one of our sons responded when I told him. "How is this possible?"

Although the cardiologist was confident, his harsh directives indicated that too much time had been lost already. He was anxious to look at Shane's arteries and take whatever measures necessary. After Shane asked a few clarifying questions, the cardiologist snapped, "Do you want to keep talking about this, or do you want me to save your life?"

Save his life, please.

Shane said his goodbyes to each of our three sons and one daughter-in-law (at the time), expressing words of love and blessing. Shane and I cried together and kissed goodbye, barely finding any words that could sum up the impact of a loving 30-year marriage.

I began pleading. *God, you can't do this to me. Please, God. I can't be a widow like my mother was. This can't be happening.*

The nurses wheeled Shane into the operating room for a standard forty-minute procedure.

As I sat in the waiting room, my emotions ranged from anger to despondency to hope. And always fear. My heart raced. I felt nauseous. For three years, I had been worrying about Shane's heart (both body and soul). I thought the weight of the ministry was going to kill him. I asked him to change his schedule and filter the input he allowed into his life. He always agreed. But we had to get through the present crisis. And then the next one. And the next one. The crises never stopped.

I watched our sons, sitting close together in the tiny waiting room, speaking in hushed tones about things that didn't interest them. Waiting for news. Barely looking at me. Maybe they could see the agony in my face.

I told myself that God was good, that he would bring us through all of this. No matter what happened, we would be fine. That's what I had always believed. But in this moment, for this brief time, faith seemed cliché. Like an embroidered pillow or a Facebook post. Of no actual use to me.

Forty minutes turned to sixty, and sixty turned to ninety, and ninety turned to hundreds. *What was taking so long? He must be alive, right? Or the surgeon would have come out?*

Three hours later, the cardiologist emerged with the news: Shane had a 95% blockage of the LAD (widow-maker) artery. He would have surely died during the night if he had gone home. It was a miracle that he had even survived the bike ride.

According to our veteran cardiologist, only one in a thousand patients survive a heart attack to the widow-maker artery if they don't get to a hospital immediately following the attack. Shane should have died on the ride. Or in his car. Or at home. Or while I drove him to the ER.

He should have become another shocking story of an athlete dropping dead, found hours later by a stranger on the side of the road.

A LIGHT IN THE DARKNESS

We love visiting the lighthouses. We enjoy climbing the winding stairs for an expansive view of the ocean. We enjoy ice cream at the local ice cream shop (there's always ice cream near lighthouses); we walk the coastline looking for shells and take selfies in front of the ocean.

The Almost-Death of A Pastor (and His Wife) | 27

Lighthouses have value for us as tourists, not as sailors. We find them picturesque but not necessary.

Every lighthouse has a unique shape, color, and pattern so that ships can easily recognize them from a distance. The lighthouse's distinctiveness tells sailors which shoreline they're facing and the dangers associated with it. Lighthouses stand in plain view on rocky peninsulas and sandy keys, warning sailors of reefs, rocks, currents, shoals, and other dangers. They also serve to guide ships into safe waters, to find channels and harbors with water deep enough to navigate.

At the top of the lighthouse is the lantern room, where the light gleams every night, giving ships enough warning to make course corrections. Before the invention of sonar or GPS navigation, lighthouse keepers walked the gallery deck and personally kept the lamps burning all night. Even today, 60-70% of lighthouses are operational. They provide a visual reference for ship captains, even those who rely on sonar and GPS.

Our body's stress signals are like a warning beacon to our souls that race through the darkness toward self-destruction. Whenever we enter dangerous waters, our warning system flashes, "Don't come this way! No safe passage here." Each of us must decide whether to view the lighthouse (the body) and its glaring lamp (the body's stress signal) as a beautiful structure or an important deterrent.

Based on our research and our personal experience, we can say unequivocally that your body is warning you about the dangers it's facing. Before Shane's heart attack, both of our bodies were signaling us about our stress and anxiety. We weren't paying attention to the beacon.

"I want to go back in," the cardiologist said to us early the next morning. "I noticed another possible spot in Shane's widow-maker yesterday, a little further down from the one we fixed. We might need to insert another stent. I couldn't leave him under any more radiation at the time."

On Shane's second day in the hospital, the cardiologist performed another heart catheterization and identified a 75% blockage just millimeters below Shane's first blockage. The first stent would have saved Shane's life for the moment, but Shane would have likely died from a second heart attack later. We would've left the hospital thinking he was good.

Because we ignored the beacons.

TO QUIT OR NOT TO QUIT?

Forty-two percent of pastors considered leaving the ministry in 2022 and 2023. That's up from the 38% following COVID. Although the trauma of the pandemic has passed, pastors still haven't recovered. Almost half are thinking about quitting the calling they trained to do. Of those considering quitting the ministry, over half (56%) cite stress as the reason. Pastors report that the stress of ministry feels overpowering. Even 34% of pastors who haven't considered leaving their jobs indicate that stress has significantly affected their calling.

In 2023, we began a podcast called *Stress Test: The Heartbeat of a Healthy Leader*. By interviewing great leaders, we wanted to learn how to better manage stress, lead through crises, and encourage other pastors to share their catalytic leadership moments. We hoped that by sharing our heart attack story, we could warn ministry leaders about the dangers of ignoring "normal" stress.

Every leader we've ever talked to (or heard about) has at least one catalytic story. Every leader has a moment when he or she decides to change because something unhealthy has happened or is about to happen. We found that pastors, pastors' wives, and non-profit leaders are concerned about personal health and ministry stress, but they often think distress is unavoidable. That's what we thought.

Pastors' answers to our stress questions are nearly universal:

- » They have thought about leaving their ministry or they think about it with frequency
- » They feel emotionally beaten up by other Christians
- » They spend an enormous amount of time handling staff problems
- » They're worried about their spouse and/or their kids
- » They regularly receive harsh or cruel criticisms over circumstances beyond their control
- » They have had serious health issues caused by stress

These are the signs of the stress that kills.

Stress always begins slowly, like normal work stress. At first, the problems seem strangely exciting to manage. People need our help! Then, we experience the weighty stress of loving people while they're suffering under addiction, grief, and pain. We give counseling, but they do not take it. We love them, but they leave our church anyway. We try our hardest, but we can't seem to make people happy.

> These are the signs of the stress that kills.

Stress feels like empathy combined with fear. We unknowingly carry the overwhelming burden of unmet expectations and disappointment. A love of serving morphs into a confusing blend of performance, resentment, and exhaustion.

We want to handle stress as Jesus handled his, but it doesn't seem possible. We must get honest about the tension to release it. More on this later.

WE DIDN'T SEE IT COMING

Within the first year of assuming the lead pastor role, I (Shane) noticed a dramatic increase in the leadership stress I was used to. I had been managing half the staff and preaching half the Sundays, but I hadn't carried the unexplainable weight of being the lead shepherd.

I began seeing doctors about my stress. No one seemed worried. Granted, I didn't often eat clean and lean, but that's why I raced road bikes and burned 2,000 calories per ride. I did triathlons and competitive running and cycling. I felt like I had a good plan for healthy living.

My physician offered an easy fix: anxiety and sleep medication. Calm your brain and get some rest. Also a cyclist, my physician assured me that I was not at risk for a heart attack because I possessed none of the physical contributing factors for heart disease. Check any that apply to you:

- ❏ Family history of heart disease
- ❏ Overweight
- ❏ Not exercising
- ❏ High blood pressure
- ❏ High cholesterol
- ❏ Rapid heart rate
- ❏ Smoker
- ❏ Abusing alcohol or drugs

"We wish everyone were as healthy as you," he always said.

Ironically, the morning following my heart attack, my cardiologist ran through this exact list of contributing factors. Do any of these apply to you?

No, no, no, no, no, no, no, no.

The cardiologist responded with surprise. "Do you have a stressful job?"

Sue and I laughed immediately and simultaneously. It was 2021.

Stress?

"Yeah," I said. "You could say that."

"Well, maybe you should change that or find another job," he said.

Huh.

That's a complicated decision. Leaving a pastorate usually means leaving your church family, your town, your kids' schools, and your friends. Pastoring opportunities don't abound everywhere, certainly not ones with a healthy DNA from the previous pastor.

Pastoring doubles as your calling, not just a job. You were called to your church.

Or at least, calling and job feel like the same thing. We think *This is what I'm meant to do. This is who I am.*

But is it?

Jesus doesn't link our calling to our identity. Our calling is simple:

» Prioritize Jesus over everything (Matthew 10:37).
» Make Jesus-followers (Matthew 28:19).

THE BIG SCARY QUESTION

When I (Shane) woke, I felt Sue's hand in mine. Her eyes were brimming with tears.

She quietly asked, "Can we be done?"

"Yes," I said. "Of course."

But I didn't know how to do that.

We didn't know how to quit the ministry. We only knew how to work harder, how to tough it out. We had not prepared ourselves for this seismic crisis of faith and practice. It was time to change everything. We knew that for sure.

HEALTHY HEARTBEATS FOR "THE ALMOST-DEATH OF A PASTOR *(and His Wife)*":

1) Write down the most stressful situations you've been through in the last five years. How have you processed the stress? Who helped you? Run the list by someone who knows you well and get their feedback on the stress you experienced during these times and how you handled it.

2) Take the "Stress Assessment" in the Resources at the back of the book.

3) Read *Zeal Without Burnout* by Christopher Ash and *The Resilient Pastor* by Glenn Packiam.

CHAPTER 2:
THE DNA OF STRESS

"Cast all your anxiety on him because he cares for you."
—1 Peter 5:7 (NIV)

We are currently writing furiously to make our fourth first-deadline for this book. Even if you don't know anything about publishing, you can tell that's not good. For someone like me (Sue), who has generally prided myself (problem #1) on meeting my writing deadlines and who is never lacking in an opinion about anything (problem #2), this little problem grew into three embarrassing emails to my very-gracious publisher.

We can't get it done on time (problem #3).

I wanted to say, "We're under a lot of stress," but that's not a great endorsement when you're writing a book on managing stress. In reality, we are living the struggle of this topic. Every. Single. Day. When you spend most of your life competing, pleasing, and performing, quitting a life of anxiety takes a monumental adjustment.

For possibly the first time in my life, I was wordless. I couldn't articulate the struggle I was undergoing; I couldn't identify and organize my thoughts. Maybe I felt ashamed. I had experienced trauma. I was probably depressed. Regardless of my desire to encourage other people on this same journey, I couldn't dig myself out of my cognitive coma or regulate my unregulated nervous system.

I had been affected by Shane's heart attack and the constant awareness of preventing another one. Shopping and food prep changed immediately. I was hyper-aware of the physical and emotional impact that certain meetings and phone calls had on Shane, on his sleep patterns, and his evening routine. And, of course, the sheer weight of ministry. The ever-present, never-ending strain of church.

My sympathetic neurology was linking my present stress to past traumas, re-igniting fear and negative thoughts. I had felt afraid before. I had felt betrayed, abandoned, and alone before. And I was feeling it again, all the time. My emotional system was shorting out, giving present hardships more importance than they deserved, yet I felt unequipped to process the realities of my stress.

I had struggled with anxiety for years without realizing it. Since I was a hard worker and a Jesus-lover, I had always pushed through my painful experiences, worked through the sleepless nights, and answered my need for perfectionism with more perfectionism (that's how perfectionists work). I could only silence my inner critic by doing more and doing it better. I found comfort in pursuing order and the practical side of life. I thought that meant I handled stress well. Limited meltdowns and high output equals healthy living.

You know your own personality and your coping mechanisms in high-stress situations. Whatever makes you feel most in control of your life will ramp up when you're in crisis in order to keep the endorphins flowing. If you're highly relational, you need the crowd and the crowd's approval even more. If you're a loner, you pull inward even more. If you're a thrill-seeker, you take bigger risks. If you're a comfort-lover, you indulge in whatever consoles you the best (food, shopping, TV, whatever).

We always self-medicate our stress. We call it good stress management. But it's not.

HOW STRESS CHANGES YOUR BIOLOGY

Jeff Bezos, founder, executive chairman, and former president of Amazon, said, "Stress comes from ignoring things which shouldn't be ignored."[1] Your body is poised to manage stress—you just need to pay attention. Your body has been biologically engineered by God to sense danger, feel fear, and spring into motion to self-protect. Whenever your mind perceives a threat, your emotional middle brain (amygdala) triggers the hypothalamus, which signals the sympathetic nervous system to respond. The stress response is instantaneous. The body protects itself in 0.9 milliseconds.

---

1 Jeff Bezos, "Stress comes from ignoring things which shouldn't be ignored," *Investors Archive*, YouTube, 13 May 2020, https://youtu.be/SQHmeRlhNtw

If you feel suddenly afraid, nervous, or vulnerable, your glands release stress hormones—adrenaline and cortisol—to protect your body through escape, fight, or camouflage. Psychologists call these the "fight/flight/freeze/fawn" responses to fear. Increased flow of blood and oxygen improves your sight and hearing, diminishes your pain, and strengthens your muscles. Your lungs expand for greater air capacity. Your digestion slows to retain the nutrients in your body. Goose pimples and hair rise on your arms and neck to improve your felt-sensory function. Your sweat stimulates greater emotive brain activity. Your blood and oxygen pump quickly into your chest cavity to support your vital organs.

That's why you feel suddenly hot, clammy, nauseous, breathy, and hyper-aware when you're stressed. Your body thinks you're under attack. It's hunkering down to protect your core.

With understanding and training, you can actually override your body's fear responses. You can slow your shallow breaths. You can calm your rapid heartbeat. You can unwind the negative spiral of your fearful thoughts. You can train your body to believe the threat has vanished. Then, your parasympathetic nervous system will signal your brain that the coast is clear. These are the skills of special forces operatives and adrenaline junkies. People who are used to fear responses teach their bodies to acclimate to fear so they can survive the threat and enjoy the thrill.

> **With understanding and training, you can actually override your body's fear responses.**

To de-stress, your brain signals your body. Your organs regulate and return to normal. We capably engage these rhythms on a normal day—during heavy traffic, bill-paying time, family arguments, work-related demands, or scary movies. God designed our bodies for normal recalibrations. God created a world of peace, unity, and love. Chaos and insecurity distort God's plan for us. He did not intend for us to live this way.

If you've developed a habit of living on adrenaline and cortisol, if you're used to working ten- to twelve-hour days, if you're sleeping five or six hours per night instead of eight, you cannot engage in life-giving practices. You won't nurture a healthy body equipped for ministry, family, or life.

Most of us are trained workaholics. We address and challenge a lifetime of beliefs, like "Good leaders are first in and last out." We produce, we mentor, we counsel, we vision-cast. We are people-oriented and task-oriented. We never stop. In response, our bodies adapt to high levels of stress hormones raging through our bodies. Like an opioid addiction, the body restructures itself to live with the new hormone levels. Future traumatic events cause the body to produce even more fear hormones. The cycle repeats itself.

Post-traumatic stress disorder (PTSD) happens because of this recalibration process; the body experiences significant trauma and remains trapped in it. Trauma is prolonged emotional distress. It doesn't matter if trauma comes from bullying or molestation—however a person accepts and processes the distress determines the lingering effects of the initial distressing incident.

We might assume that PTSD only happens to victims or witnesses of violence. I (Sue) discovered that PTSD can happen to anyone. Disruptive life events that go untreated create a continued stressful trauma that debilitates us and diminishes our impact.

Whenever we ignore hurt, it can become trauma. Past trauma builds and entwines itself into whatever might be happening in the moment. When the anniversary of my mom's death came during the writing process of this book, that grief interlaced with current stress and pain; my body reacted to the stress in the form of sickness, body aches, high anxiety, depression, and crippling pain. Trauma can trigger grief and vice versa, layer upon layer.

Everyone has different levels of resilience and support. And if we're Christ-followers, we have the Holy Spirit. The Great Physician. The Comforter. We have exactly who and what we need. But we still panic. We despair. We strategize to handle the weight we carry and the problems we encounter.

Shane and I are still learning about leadership stress and how to manage it. Today, Shane stopped home at lunchtime for a breather. His watch had registered a low HRV (heart rate variability), so he came home to recalibrate. Heart rate variability, oversimplified, is the amount of oxygen in your bloodstream between heartbeats.

Shane's watch tracks his HRV and warns him when his body contacts a situation creating low levels of space and air between heartbeats. Low levels of oxygen equals high levels of stress and stress hormones. High HRV means peaceful and happy—lots of oxygen between heartbeats.

Low HRV means he practices deep breathing. He sits outside or goes to the river. He reads Scripture and listens to worship. He sits with me.

That's not always doable on a meeting-packed workday, but surviving a heart attack dictates that he finds the time. Five minutes in a worship-filled office brings down his HRV. He no longer prides himself on pushing through or pretending to be indestructible. He postpones his next meeting five or ten minutes, and he adjusts everything.

His body responds. More air. Longer breaths. Cooler body temperature. Lower heart rate. Calmer mood.

WHEN YOUR CALLING CREATES STRESS

Like many of you, we've waded through a few years of debilitating depression, significant post-traumatic stress, and several not-so-healthy coping mechanisms. We have wanted to give up on God's calling. For that matter, we have doubted we followed the right calling at all. Did we hear wrong? Maybe we weren't following God's voice. Why would he lead us through such deep waters? We're trying to serve him.

Paul describes his struggle in 1 Corinthians 9:16-18: "For when I preach the gospel, I cannot boast, since I am compelled to preach. Woe to me if I do not preach the gospel! If I preach voluntarily, I have a reward; if not voluntarily, I am simply discharging the trust committed to me. What then is my reward? Just this: that in preaching the gospel I may offer it free of charge, and so not make full use of my rights as a preacher of the gospel."

WHEN THE CIRCUITS TRIP

Stress is not wrong. It's not unhealthy or sinful.

It's just a signal. Stress is God's natural switch for biological function, the breaker in our body's breaker box that flips whenever we overload the circuits.

Our house was built in 1958. After we bought it from a very elderly couple, we found out that the house's outlets were 2-pronged. In addition to the outlet situation, the whole kitchen, living room, and sunroom were wired to a single breaker in the breaker box. If we used an electric skillet and microwave at the same time, the breaker tripped. *It's too much for me,* said the kitchen wiring. *I can't handle it.*

We had to understand and accept one crucial reality for cooking in our yet-to-be-rewired kitchen: our kitchen could not handle the same workload that other kitchens could handle. It could handle what it could handle. Our job, if we wanted to cook, was managing the electrical currents of our unique kitchen so we could cook without losing our minds.

That's what stress is like. We all have individual electrical currents and wiring systems unique to us. When our fear breaker trips, we have to make adjustments to move forward. We can't just flip the breaker back on and plug all the same appliances back into all the outlets at the same time and expect everything to work. The circuit breaker is just going to trip again.

Stress signals you to manage your electrical currents. You must identify the clues: the rapid heart rate, the hyper-awareness, the toxic thoughts and manic conclusions, the sweaty foreheads, the seizing stomach pain. Your body always tells you what your mind believes. The more you ignore the signs, the more intricately your mind interlaces with your memories, even subdued or unconscious memories. The body remembers fear. Not logic. Not vision. Not restoration. Fear.

(No wonder God instructed the Israelites to erect monuments to him to mark every significant spiritual victory. He knew they would remember their fear but forget his rescue.)

Life events will vary in severity and consequence, but the amygdala doesn't know the difference. Panic feels the same. Betrayal feels the same. Abandonment feels the same. Hopelessness feels the same.

If you experience trauma and you don't address your stress triggers in a healthy way, your stress will morph into anxiety. The devil loves anxiety because it deconstructs your faith and cripples you. Anxiety preys on your natural fears and your unrealistic phobias.

> If you experience trauma and you don't address your stress triggers in a healthy way, your stress will morph into anxiety.

You might assume that hard work and medication can hold you together for your teams, your family, or yourself. Not true. When you don't admit and address your anxiety, everyone around you begins paying for it. If you, as a leader, are not healthy, your staff will develop an atmosphere of unhealthy stress. Negative emotions become embedded in your culture through lies about performance and identity. Even scarier, stress negatively affects our families. Even if your spouse or kids don't complain about it, they can feel your stress.

STOP STEPPING OVER THE ROPE

Counselor and psychotherapist Jeremy J. Lanning explains tension and stress with an illustration from his years in the U.S. Navy. Sailors were taught to step on ropes, not over ropes. Every rope that crisscrosses an aircraft carrier holds thousands of pounds. Ropes flex with the constant movement of the ship. If a sailor is stepping on a rope when it breaks, the tension will throw him, possibly seriously injuring him. But if that sailor is stepping over a rope that snaps, the pressure can cut him in half.

Your stress is like a rope holding a ship together. Stepping over it is ignoring it, to your own peril. Stepping on the rope is recognizing it and respecting the danger that it suggests. Don't step over the signals your stress is sending you. Acknowledge your stress and step on it.

Is anyone in your family having trouble with

- Sleep
- Stomach aches
- Nightmares
- Identity or self-esteem
- Food-related issues, like binging or purging
- Significant weight gain or weight loss
- Bitterness or envy
- Trouble concentrating or learning
- Relationships
- Anger, resentment, or blame-shifting
- Self-harming
- Muscle aches, body pains
- Unusual amount of crying or sobbing
- High blood pressure

If these symptoms exist in you or your family members, take some time to analyze the stressors in your life. If you haven't done it yet, take the "Stress Assessment" and "Finding the Source of Your Stress" located in the Resources section in the back of the book. We always encourage seeing a professional counselor or therapist, especially one licensed in trauma or cognitive therapy.

Our counseling meetings are possibly the most important meetings we have each week.

We all need an objective perspective to help us recognize our behaviors as symptomatic of something significant; we need help to implement a solution.

WHAT'S KILLING PASTORS (AND THEIR SPOUSES)?

The aftermath of COVID produced some shocking numbers about pastors and their personal health. According to many research organizations,

- » Pastors average between 50-75 work hours per week,
- » Stress is a pastor's top mental health problem,
- » 43% of pastors "feel lonely and isolated," and
- » In spite of stress and burnout, 47% of pastors "can't see doing anything else".

Pastoring could be killing us, and we're not sure how to stop it.

ENTER THE SPOUSE'S STRESS

I began carrying both Shane's stress and mine. Shane didn't ask me to carry his stress. I just couldn't separate myself from it. I worried obsessively, making unhelpful demands and suggestions. I became something of an insomniac, sometimes only sleeping four hours per night. The exhaustion and stress made me unproductive and edgy.

I watched my husband grow depressed and frustrated. He took endless phone calls and read horribly hurtful emails. His shoulders slumped. He couldn't fall asleep. I pumped him for information and reacted in mama-bear fashion to the problems he faced. My reactions created more anxiety for him. Unable to problem-solve or speak to anyone about our stress, I internalized it, becoming angry, depressed, and resentful.

I began having a series of physical problems—infections, aches, and pains—nothing too serious, but always something. I planned occasional getaways for us so we could breathe and recoup. The stress followed us, or if we were lucky, it waited at home for our return, like a pile of bills or hundreds of emails in our inboxes.

Our bodies adapted to running at a fear-driven, adrenalin-heavy new normal. We believed if we just held on a little longer, everything would work out. We called it faith, but it wasn't. Faith doesn't wear you down. It holds you up.

We bought into some leadership lies. *If I can't handle the stress, I'm not a great leader. Work harder. Push forward. Be an example. Carry the load for everyone. Listen to the criticisms and the complaining. Meet people's needs. Sacrifice your personal time; cut your vacation short. Inspire, coach, challenge, marry, bury. That's servant leadership. That's what good pastors do. We're here to serve everyone first, to be the good shepherd, to be Jesus.*

But this is not healthy servant leadership. This is death by pastoring.

(You're not Jesus, and that's not how he led.)

HEALTHY HEARTBEATS FOR "THE DNA OF STRESS":

1) Ask yourself: What causes your heart rate to go up? What situations or people make you panic? Get help to eliminate, delegate, or get assistance.

2) Read *The Self-Aware Leader* by John Maxwell.

3) Slowly read and process the research and therapies in *The Body Keeps the Score* by Bessel Van Der Kolk, M.D.

4) Consider buying an Oura ring and monitoring your HRV.

5) Practice yoga, stretching, spiritual meditation, deep breathing. These practices calm down your parasympathetic nervous system.

6) Look at your schedule. Limit the amount of adversarial or stressful meetings you have each day and each week. Choose the minimum that you can emotionally handle, and stick to your limit.

CHAPTER 3:
WHAT WE DIDN'T LEARN IN SEMINARY

"Anxiety weighs down the heart, but a kind word cheers it up."
—Proverbs 12:25

We learned to work in seminary. We learned Greek and Hebrew; we became skilled with the lexicon and concordance. We learned how to speed-read thousands of pages and crank out theology papers in a weekend. We learned that working and taking seminary courses meant late nights and lots of caffeine (or sugar), grumpy mornings, and brain fog.

We had already developed an insatiable appetite for the Word of God; seminary fueled the flame. We grew intimate with Scripture and marveled at its newness and power. We applied the Living Word to our scholarly ministry-junkie lives, believing that seminary had prepared us for the real world of ministry.

Maybe, like parenting, we thought we knew what we were doing until we actually started doing it. "Comparing data from

2015 and 2020, Barna found that pastors across the nation were facing a shocking surge in perceived gaps in their own training."[2] For example, 27% felt underprepared to handle conflict in 2015, but 40% felt underprepared in 2020. Statistical increases were similar concerning managing church politics and training leaders.

All of us who spent the time and money on seminary believed that our training was critical (and it is), so we sacrificed and studied and graduated. But nothing we studied prepared us for the real stress of ministry: people.

We weren't ready for the load of carrying people's burdens and the attached spiritual weight. We didn't learn how to hire and fire staff without creating more crises. We talked about a work/life balance, but we have constantly struggled with the tension of living it out. We never learned how to graciously handle power plays from influential members. We didn't learn how to correct and restore staff after significant spiritual failures or how to help our team members retire when they could no longer work but couldn't afford to leave. We didn't learn how to navigate legal implications, bylaws, building projects, or insurance and retirement funding during an economic downturn. We could never have anticipated navigating a pandemic or race wars or national grief.

Seminary training didn't address the massive stress associated with stylistic changes, cultural shifts, or adjusting a DNA that's gone sideways. We never learned the value of consistent

---

[2] "7-Year Trends: Pastors Feel More Loneliness and Less Support," *Barna Research*, 12 July 2023, https://www.barna.com/research/pastor-support-systems/

professional therapy and counseling for pastors. We didn't consider how a pastor and spouse might struggle to find intimate, trustworthy friendships within the church. Nobody considered that ministry marriages would suffer for reasons other than infidelity. It turns out that

- » 65% of pastors feel lonely,
- » 69% of pastors' wives have no trusted confidantes,
- » 50% of pastors' wives distrust church members to be their friends,
- » 70% of pastors do not have a close friend, and
- » 38% are divorced or divorcing.

The Church has a generation of leaders who don't think they're going to make it.

WHAT'S GOING TO TAKE YOU OUT

One of my (Sue's) master's classes addressed ministry pain. My professor, author A. J. Swoboda, unpacked the benefits of pain in his book *A Glorious Dark*. "Pain isn't good because it's painful. Pain can be good because it makes us all philosophers and theologians—it forces all of us to come face-to-face with ultimate reality. Pain destroys superficiality."[3]

Cognitively, we understand that life and ministry bring pain. Subconsciously, we probably expect God to exempt us from pain. It's easy to forget that pain is a magnifying glass to our faith; the greater the suffering, the greater the testimony and God's glory.

---

3 A. J. Swoboda, *A Glorious Dark*, Baker Books, 2014, 73.

We claim "for me to live is Christ, and to die is gain," but when a betrayal or catastrophe occurs, it's natural to doubt the validity of God's goodness. Pain and faith do not actually oppose one another; rather, pain exposes the depth and reality of our faith. In Philippians, the context of faith and contentment is pain with suffering. Pain because of suffering and suffering because of ministry. Paul's not going to survive his persecution; he's going to die for the cause of Christ. There's nothing superficial about his faith or his reality.

> Pain exposes the depth and reality of our faith.

Pastors in the Western Church ministry don't often grapple with this concept until they've been knee-deep in pastoring for a while. When you're young in the ministry, there's an undefinable energy that comes from experiencing pain with people and for people—of rushing to the hospital to pray with someone in the middle of the night. Of weeping with parents over a child. Of pleading with a husband and wife suffering from the pain of infidelity. We even find some satisfaction in clocking long hours and existing on caffeine and sugar.

Certainly, mercy is a spiritual gift. Compassion comes from the Holy Spirit. But it only takes a little ministry experience to realize that celebrating suffering, apart from humility and supernatural Spirit-filling, dictates a life of self-pity and willful martyrdom. Martyrs don't live; they die. Anyone who plays the martyr suffers to bring glory to himself.

In seminary, we didn't talk about the perils of ministry martyrdom. We couldn't wait to suffer with people! We didn't understand the inevitable toll of leadership pain and stress. Perhaps we weren't listening well. Or perhaps our professors omitted the dark side of leadership as they sought to build effective, energetic leaders who expanded the church and the kingdom of God. None of us anticipated wanting to quit when we didn't want to quit.

Pastors are not the quitting kind of people. We want to endure. We haven't lost our faith. We're not angry at God. But most of us are way burned out. That's probably why you're reading this book. You're burned out, afraid of burning out, or know someone who is burned out. You're wondering how much longer you can hang on and if you should. You wonder if hanging on makes you a terrible pastor. That's your reality.

WHAT DOES THIS MEAN FOR ME?

Leaving your current ministry may ultimately be God's call for your next step. But leaving your ministry in crisis means you take your crisis with you, and the church becomes the reason you left. And then you still have to get healthy anyway.

Carey Neiwhof states that the average pastor only stays in one place for three to seven years. There's no point in putting down roots and loving people if you're leaving in a few years.

Pastoring creates isolation and hesitant personal relationships. Three to seven years is not enough time to see transformation in a church. Tack on the trauma of putting your kids in new schools, figuring out a new culture, and picking up the baggage left by the last pastor. Pastoring can become a traumatic and transient experience.

Many pastors solve the problem of uprooting their families by leaving one church and taking a position at another church in town. This solution comes with additional problems: church splits or shifts, awkward encounters (or avoidance) of old relationships, gossip around the city, and more isolation.

Leaving your ministry might be your next contextual calling, but your "what's next" is likely more complex. John Maxwell likes to say, "If you are going to be successful in life, you don't leave something. You go to something!"

TRAINING FOR THE RACE

Going the distance in ministry takes tenacity, endurance, and focus. God might move you from one ministry to another, but he never leads you away from your designed calling.

In Philippians 3:13-14, Paul uses the metaphor of racing to encourage the Philippians toward the singular focus of steady spiritual growth in the midst of confusion about their suffering. "But one thing I do: Forgetting what is behind and straining toward what is ahead, I press on toward the goal to win the prize for which God has called me heavenward in Christ Jesus."

I (Shane) love this passage. I'm a racer. It makes sense to me.

In my mid-thirties, I realized that if I didn't participate in a competitive sport, I wouldn't ever exercise again. I could no longer keep up with 20-somethings on a soccer field. I discovered that races scratched my competitive itch and made me get out there and exercise.

One summer, my friend Buck, an experienced triathlete, inspired me to join him in training for a sprint triathlon (the shortest triathlon distance). The competition, not the training, compelled me, and I caught the racing bug. We began running 10Ks and marathons together. Then we did larger triathlons, like Olympic and half-Ironmans. Then, we picked the full Ironman that we wanted to do.

An Ironman distance is a 2.5-mile open-water swim, followed by a 112-mile bike race, followed by a marathon. It's exquisite torture. (Maybe a little like pastoring.)

Buck had done several Ironmans already, so he knew what he was doing. He put me on a training schedule, which is important for muscle-building, endurance, and injury prevention. His strategy was to hit peak athletic performance on race day, not before or after. I trained gradually for months, every week increasing mileage and taking off the prescribed rest or recovery days. Many competitors train and compete to qualify for a bigger race event; they are determined to break records or win races. Athletes like me just train to finish.

By the month of the Ironman event, I was logging two training sessions per day and about 20 hours per week. Sue tells me that at an Ironman finish line, nearly every racer and fan cries. Weeps, even. The finish is an emotionally moving experience. Competitors literally stumble across the finish line, shaking, emaciated, pasty, even vomiting, falling down. Somewhere along the race route, the bodies of these endurance athletes have started shutting down from the stress of pushing themselves beyond their natural limitations. Although endurance athletes might have an appetite for pain, I think most racers have a greater thirst for completion. They want to finish well more than they fear the suffering. My goal—my prize—was finishing in under 12 hours. It was a big commitment for my first Ironman. My race was pure agony, but I did it. I couldn't wait to hear the announcer say, "Shane Schlesman, you are an Ironman."

Well done, good and faithful servant.

The Greek word for *servant* in Matthew 25:21 is *doulos*, meaning "bondsman." It's the male version of the word "servant" or "bondswoman" that Mary uses in Luke 1:38 when she accepts her call as Jesus' mother. We get our English word *doula* from this word. Mary literally calls herself the *doula* for Jesus—she recognizes her role of bringing him into the world, a servant for the miracle of incarnation. She does not see herself as a mother with rights to his attention. A true *doulos* serves the needs of his master and relinquishes any personal ambition. Like a pastor.

ADDRESSING THE MENTAL GAME

Let's keep the racing/pastoring analogy going a little longer. Good training is strategic. It involves diet and routine and body chemistry, pace, and planning. But the actual race, while incorporating all of that, involves a harder piece, the one that each racer develops during all those training sessions without even realizing it. The hardest part of a race isn't struggling for air in dark water, tucking and pedaling into a headwind for endless hours, or hydrating a body completely that's depleted of water and salt. The hardest part isn't even the immense suffering of a body shutting down.

The hardest part is making it to the start line of the race. You have to balance the mental and physical strain to even get there. If you overtrain, you get injured. If you don't rest correctly, you get injured. If you undertrain, you won't finish the race. You train so you can finish the race. You train your will to keep going and not give up. To fight the thoughts that you can't do it, you weren't built for this, you're going to die.

This is what your training teaches you, what suffering always teaches you: you can make it. You're going to finish this.

> This is what your training teaches you, what suffering always teaches you: you can make it. You're going to finish this.

Paul explained the importance of training to the church at Corinth:

"Do you not know that in a race all the runners run, but only one gets the prize? Run in such a way as to get the prize. Everyone who

competes in the games goes into strict training. They do it to get a crown that will not last, but we do it to get a crown that will last forever. Therefore, I do not run like someone running aimlessly; I do not fight like a boxer beating the air. No, I strike a blow to my body and make it my slave so that after I have preached to others, I myself will not be disqualified for the prize" (1 Corinthians 9:24-27).

You are going to make it. We are going to make it.

DON'T RUN AIMLESSLY

Leadership stress is not unique to pastors, but pastoral leadership is unique.

- » Pastoring carries the spiritual weight of souls in addition to organizational and functional responsibilities.
- » Pastoring carries natural expectations that Christian people will behave better than lost people.
- » Pastoring has inconsistent "rules for engagement." Physicians and counselors have licensing rules; teachers have the standards of learning, the teachers' union, and their school boards; law enforcement has the law. But according to counselor and psychotherapist Jeremy Lanning, LPC, CCTP, ministry is "the wild-west of the helping professions."[4] Conflict resolution, discipline, theology, and accountability vary according to individual church contexts.

Seminary may not completely prepare us for ministry, yet ministry unmasks the eternal struggle between the cause of Christ and the enemy of our souls. God wants us to finish the

---

[4] Jeremy J. Lanning, LPC, CCTP, *Conversation*, 14 Nov. 2023.

race marked out for us, the race he intends for us to win. We may not be able to live a stress-free life, but we can live free from the grip of stress.

HEALTHY HEARTBEATS FOR "WHAT WE DIDN'T LEARN IN SEMINARY":

1) Whether or not you attended seminary, what preconceived ideas did you have about pastoring before you became a pastor? How have you processed the reality of pastoring?

2) Find a Christian counselor. To help facilitate vulnerability and safety, we recommend tele-health or finding counselors who aren't familiar with your church. You need to be able to speak freely.

3) Read *The 21 Irrefutable Laws of Leadership* by John Maxwell and *A Glorious Dark* by A. J. Swoboda.

CHAPTER 4:

THE SNARE OF EXPECTATIONS

*"Hope deferred makes the heart sick, but
a longing fulfilled is a tree of life."*
—Proverbs 13:12

My (Shane's) first job after college was managing a paint department in a local hardware store. I didn't know anything about paint, but I could sell. I had great ideas about improving and expanding the paint department. However, I soon learned that customers only cared about finding paint color samples where they always had been.

Regardless of my vision, the management wanted me to run the department the same way the previous guy had run it.

And when the previous guy wanted to return to the store, guess what happened to me?

They let me go. They valued keeping everything the same as it had always been more than moving forward.

When I went into the insurance industry for the freedom and the bonus structure, I found a similar impasse. Although we had award systems and huge bonuses, our pay and performance markers revolved around a structure and value system that hadn't changed much in the last century. Regardless of changes in the market, target demographic, and culture, my boss expected me to conduct business the way it had always been done.

Eventually, I shifted to outside sales consulting for greater earning potential and flexibility for my family and ministry schedules. Even though I was an independent consultant leading the company in sales—even though my boss got a cut from all my revenue I generated—my boss was irritated that I spent my personal time running a campus ministry as a volunteer instead of drinking with my clients.

It seemed that for all the corporate talk about change and improvement, everyone felt more comfortable with traditions.

I could not wait to be paid for work with eternal value. When I left behind my insurance agency, residual income, and all the perks of being a top sales associate, Sue and I embraced full-time ministry with excitement and faith. Finally, we had escaped production and performance. No more expectations to be someone we weren't designed to be!

(Cue the laughter.)

THE BUSINESS OF CHURCH

Spoiler: we did not escape expectations by entering the ministry. If we have learned nothing else from the pandemic and the chaos that ensued after it, we have learned that there are expectations associated with spiritual care that we can never meet. People have the expectation that you will not only agree with their perspectives but you will condone, support, and celebrate how they think and act.

In *Overcoming the Dark Side of Leadership,* Gary McIntosh and Samuel Rima write, "When our expectations are unrealistic or become selfishly motivated, they can become very destructive in the life of the person toward whom they are directed... expectations can either propel people to achieve or they can produce pain and failure."[5] The proof, as they said, is in the pudding: if you are experiencing pain with feelings of failure, there's a good chance you or someone else has levied unrealistic expectations on you, and you are buckling under the weight of stress.

In Exodus 15, Jethro brought Moses' wife and sons to meet Moses in the wilderness; Jethro saw the unrealistic expectations that were weighing Moses down. Moses had personally committed to listening to every person's problems. Jethro said to him, "'What you are doing is not good. You and these people who come to you will only wear yourselves out. The work is too heavy for you; you cannot handle it alone. Listen now to me and I will give you some advice, and may God be with you.'" (Exodus 18:17-19). Moses followed Jethro's advice. He delegated and focused his attention on his specific calling: to be God's representative and teach his decrees. He let someone else do everything else.

---

[5] Gary L. McIntosh and Samuel D. Rima, *Overcoming the Dark Side of Leadership*, Baker Books, 2007, 185.

> Share your stress with a wise person who can give you perspective. Learn to delegate.

HOW TO HANDLE DISAPPOINTMENTS

We are not good at handling expectations yet. Disappointment stings. We care what people think and how our organization works. But we are learning that expectations come from earthly thinking. God knows that we are dust; he expects nothing from us. He only woos us to himself out of love.

Sam Chand talks about two ways to handle hurt and disappointment in his book *Leadership Pain*. Sam first finds "pain partners," people he chooses, friends who can help him process his leadership pain; they don't solve his problems or minimize his hurt. They let him verbalize his disappointment without judging him. Secondly, Sam recalls God's faithfulness to him in the past. God is good, God has been good, and God is doing good even when we can't see it. Perhaps this is the reason that Paul recounts God's faithfulness so frequently in his letters; he continually suffers from leadership pain but realizes the power of recounting God's faithfulness.

Let's look at how some great Biblical leaders handled expectations.

» David: Attack the problem, not the people. The Amalekites looted David's towns, Ziklag and Negev, and carried off the wives and children of David's army. David and his men wept together, and then David's soldiers talked about stoning him to death. Adversity can quickly turn loyal friends into vengeful enemies. Instead of asserting his authority, David sought the Lord's wisdom and invited his men to join him in pursuing their enemies and bringing back their families. David had compassion for his men's pain and perspective but quickly attacked the real enemy.

» Moses: Nurture God's favor above popular opinion. Every time the Israelites murmured against God or Moses in the wilderness, Moses interceded for them and secured God's mercy. We know that Moses valued horizontal relationships: he asked God to let Aaron join him in his calling; he pleaded to God for Miriam's life, even though her offense was against Moses' wife Zipporah; Moses continually showed compassion for the complaining Israelites. Often, Moses stood alone in his vision, yet for the most part, he prioritized his relationship with God over his own popularity. At the risk of his life, he valued standing in God's presence, being close to him, and hearing his voice, even if that meant he was alone.

» Elijah: Obey God implicitly. During a famine, when the king's men searched throughout the country for Elijah, the prophets all hid. For three and a half years, God asked Elijah to trust him: from a flowing brook to a starving widow to a dead child, God used increasingly difficult circumstances to incrementally grow Elijah's faith in God's provision. Elijah witnessed great miracles—and was the implementer of great miracles—because he obeyed God immediately when God told him to do something.

THE LIE OF EXPECTATION

Here's the problem with expectations (besides the obvious stress that expectations carry). Embedded in expectation is a root of self-preservation. When we expect people to know what we want and how we want it, we disobey the second Greatest Commandment, "Love your neighbor as yourself." On the receiving end, when we cater to expectations, we disobey the first Greatest Commandment, "Love the Lord your God with all your heart, with all your soul, and with all your mind."

Expectations are profoundly unbiblical. God expects nothing from us; He demands our obedience but gives us freedom of choice. He designs our paths and gives us freedom for creativity. He restores our souls and gives us freedom to love. He redeems our mistakes and gives us freedom to make amends. He heals our diseases and gives us freedom for gratefulness. He comforts us in our grief and gives us freedom to process.

> Expectations are profoundly unbiblical.

Obedience is the gateway to freedom, not the locked door of independence and individuality. The devil has spent the history of mankind convincing humans to believe that obedience is enslavement. He accomplishes that through entitlement-based expectation, which creates a platform for disappointment.

He fuels his strategy with lies: if we mess up, God must be disappointed with us. If we can't get our church to grow, God must be disappointed with us. If popular opinion turns against us, God must be disappointed with us.

Truth: God loves you exactly the same as if you were popular, successful, or respected. You are created in his image, and he is in the process of restoring you to your original state: physical, mental, emotional, and spiritual perfection. The lie embedded in production creates a performance-driven value system.

God doesn't need us to do anything. He doesn't even need us. He wants us.

God's kingdom runs opposite of this world. We value performance, results, appreciation, acknowledgment, reward, process, structure. God values people, growth, and transformation. He's always about reaching our souls. His purposes take the sting out of personality hang-ups, giftedness, opportunity, platform, everything.

Let God transform your mind and heart. He will change your business, your ministry, your family, your friendships, your mental health. A soul that thirsts for God does not feel the weight of expectation. Therefore, it doesn't perform. It doesn't feel disappointed. It just exists in a state of worship. We are free to choose the better things; unlike Martha (who did so many important things), we become listening souls like Mary (who had nothing to do).

King Saul is so full of anxiety that he's throwing spears and hunting down his loyal son-in-law. But David, hiding in the caves of Ein-Gedi, can direct his anxiety to the Lord by composing psalms of praise and worship. David writes in Psalm 42:1-5:

As the deer pants for streams of water, so my soul pants for you, my God. My soul thirsts for God, for the living God. When can I go and meet with God? My tears have been my food day and night, while people say to me all day long, "Where is your God?" These things I remember as I pour out my soul: how I used to go to the house of God under the protection of the Mighty One with shouts of joy and praise among the festive throng. Why, my soul, are you downcast? Why so disturbed within me? Put your hope in God, for I will yet praise him, my Savior and my God.

THE WEIGHT OF EXPECTATION

Anne Lamott writes, "Expectations are resentments waiting to happen."[6] Human nature directs us toward resentment because stress germinates in the soil of expectation. God designed us to

---

[6] Anne Lamott, as quoted in *Rising Strong: The Reckoning. The Rumble. The Revolution.* by Brené Brown, Random House, 4 April 2017, 140.

work, to be productive. In Genesis 2, God's curse on mankind is an unhealthy tension regarding work. Post-fall, mankind is engineered to produce under the weight of expectation, identity, and self-worth. Because we fail to meet our own expectations, we allow performance to creep into our perspectives and corrode our work.

We all pray for God's blessing and power, but we're still surprised when things don't work out according to our expectations. Brené Brown writes in *Rising Strong,* "Disappointment is unmet expectations. The more significant the expectations, the more significant the disappointment."[7]

Why do we allow ourselves to be disappointed by God, the God who left heaven to die for us? He has nothing left to prove, but we expect him to keep proving his love to us.

THE SOLUTION TO EXPECTATION

Values keep us consistent and constant in our ministry. Known values prevent misaligned expectations and disappointment. As leaders, we're constantly struggling to improve culture, cast vision, and execute God's mission. As we manage the tension between what worked in the past and what needs to change for the future, we have to keep our personal (and corporate) values central to our actions. Value-driven leadership impedes anxiety and fear because our focus is on the why, not the how or what.

John Maxwell addresses the importance of value-driven leadership for managing stress like this: "Values not only help

---

[7] Brené Brown, *Rising Strong,* 139.

people to live better, but they also help people to stay true to themselves. Life is a marathon, not a sprint. You have to be able to sustain yourself, to keep yourself going, to continue pursuing your vision."[8]

Recently, our church staff read a book that challenged us to re-examine our staff culture and identify any toxic practices. As our staff sat in discussion groups, we had to answer the question, "What is our church's primary value?"

Of course, we immediately touted our successes with discipleship, missions, and worship. We have a great church with a great history. But in the context of the question, the real answer to this question isn't found in our history or theology. It's found in our practice. Consider these questions to find your primary values (either corporate or personal):

- » What are you willing to fight to achieve?
- » What do you defend?
- » What are you willing to suffer for?
- » What are your non-negotiables?
- » Where do you spend your time and money?
- » What do you dream about—what would you do if anything were possible?

Ask value-based questions to find your debilitating stress. Remember, anxiety grows in climates of inconvenience and discomfort. But discomfort is imperative for growth. You can't control what other people do, but you can take out your sword of

---

[8] John Maxwell, *Change Your World*, Harper Collins, 2021, 118.

truth and start cutting away the scar tissue caused by unresolved conflict and perfectionism. Cut away anything that has accumulated from disease and neglect, anything that isn't directly feeding the mission of God (sharing the gospel and making disciples). The sideways energy of being more and doing more generates a culture of stress.

Everything we do and the way we do it reflects the value we assign to it. The higher the priority in time and mental energy, the higher the personal value for this area.

Do any of these signs of ignored values apply to you?

- » You feel like your schedule is controlling your life
- » You don't have time for things that bring you joy
- » Most of your time goes to tasks, not people
- » You don't feel like yourself anymore
- » You struggle to manage negative thought patterns
- » You feel protective over what you accomplish or make excuses for what you don't accomplish
- » You feel anxiety, chaos, and distress in your body or spirit
- » You're not fulfilling the dreams you had for yourself
- » You feel like you've missed God's calling on your life
- » You engage in secretive, manipulative, or controlling behavior to get things done
- » You think about self-harm and/or ways to escape your life
- » You're not spending most of your time in your areas of giftedness

THE WARNING OF EXPECTATION

David is a natural leader and a passionate pursuer of intimacy. His values drive his behavior. While David's heart is his greatest strength, unguarded, it contributes to his downfall. He allows his values to change; his passion for God morphs into pleasure for himself. David's son Solomon would later write, "Above all else, guard your heart, for everything you do flows from it" (Proverbs 4:23).

Be aware of others' expectations because they create stress through

- » An unholy attachment to process. Wrong things seem right when you value acclaim. A cycle of expectation and disappointment create an unhealthy stress spiral for pastors; if your identity and the success of the ministry depend on your ability to please your congregation, you are headed for disaster.
- » An unsustainable attachment to personality. Providing constant attention creates unhealthy leadership environments where people expect direct access and immediate care. Even Jesus didn't meet needs all the time.
- » An unrealistic commitment to responsibility. Leaders often take on too much responsibility because it's easier and more efficient to do the work themselves. You have the most training and experience, but the work of the ministry should be done mostly by your lay people. The rule of delegation states that when people are 70% ready for a job, that's when you give them authority and

responsibility. We all learn from making mistakes. Let your people make mistakes.

Teams that feel the pressure to work as hard or as perfectly as their stressed-out leader become an organization of workaholics. Staff will resent or envy their leader's time off rather than celebrate it; consequently, pastors won't take necessary vacations and sabbaticals, or they will take them begrudgingly. In high-expectation cultures, leaders work harder and/or worry that people won't think they're working hard enough. Deception easily grows in a culture of workaholism and performance because leaders must keep the expectation satisfied, at least on the surface.

As a leader, you must continue to grow and develop apart from the expectations of others. Analyze the source of your debilitating stress and unshackle yourself from it. Call stress what it is:

» Fear.
» Anxiety.
» Expectation.
» Pride.

Let's dismantle the snares that stress creates.

HEALTHY HEARTBEATS FOR
"THE SNARE OF EXPECTATION":

1) What tasks that you currently manage do you have to do? If you ignore tradition and expectation, which responsibilities should you delegate?

2) Identify your top three spiritual gifts. How do you activate these for the benefit of the body? Now, set up a plan for off-loading everything else.

3) Read *Resilient* by John Eldredge and subscribe to his "Pause" App. Do the mental and physical breathing exercises.

4) Read *The Gifts of Imperfection* or *Atlas of the Heart* by Brené Brown. While not Christian books, you will be astounded at the spiritual applications you can make as you read them.

5) What difficult decisions are you currently making? Identify the core value that feeds your fear. Meditate on God's truth and adjust your values, if necessary.

CHAPTER 5:
A BOTTOMLESS PIT

"Like lions they open their jaws against me, roaring and tearing into their prey. My life is poured out like water, and all my bones are out of joint. My heart is like wax, melting within me. My strength has dried up like sunbaked clay. My tongue sticks to the roof of my mouth. You have laid me in the dust and left me for dead. . . . O Lord, do not stay far away! You are my strength; come quickly to my aid!"
—Psalm 22:13-15, 19

THE ANXIETY EPIDEMIC

Anxiety disorders are the most common mental health concern in the United States. Over 40 million adults in the U.S. (19%) have an anxiety disorder. In the last ten years, anxiety disorders have increased 13%.[9]

Anxiety and worry are not the same. Anxiety is emotional; worry is thinking. Worry operates in the prefrontal cortex, where

---

[9] "Anxiety Disorders," National Alliance on Mental Health, https://www.nami.org/About-Mental-Illness/Mental-Health-Conditions/Anxiety-Disorders

you problem-solve and ask "if/then" questions. You assess danger here and assign your fears their due mental energy.

> Anxiety disorders are the most common mental health concern in the United States.

Anxiety lives in your middle brain, where you operate from your emotions, where whatever you're feeling seems to be true. Because it's emotional, anxiety causes your thoughts to spiral. Anxiety debilitates; it persists regardless of the reality or likelihood of danger. Because of its persistence, anxiety elicits the same biological reactions in your body that fear does; your body can't differentiate between emotional reality and illusion.

God gives us the tools to avoid, conquer, and redeem anxiety. "See, I am doing a new thing! Now it springs up; do you not perceive it? I am making a way in the wilderness and streams in the wasteland" (Isaiah 43:19). God walks with us through the desert places and carves out canyons, fills them with water, and refreshes our dry, dark places. The places we hide. The places we excuse. The places we accept, even though they are dousing the fire God has put in our hearts.

Since our behaviors, emotions, and thoughts begin with belief, let's address the heart issue; it's the center of who you are. "Search me, God, and know my heart; test me and know my anxious thoughts. See if there is any offensive way in me and lead me in the way everlasting" (Psalm 139:23-24). Your soul and spirit yearn for God. Your soul must be filled by him or else be eternally empty.

It's silly to tell ourselves that we don't have a heart problem simply because we teach and preach for others to search their hearts. We are perhaps more gifted at covering up heart problems than the average person because we spend so much time doing good deeds.

Let's do the brave work. Let's trace our desires, fears, and disappointments back to the source. Let's identify the problem, give it to God, and let him transform our hearts and minds in Christ Jesus.

First Peter 5 contains one of the countless passages that address the marriage of the heart, mind, soul, and spirit. Peter, in his succinct and straightforward way, writes a compelling argument for breaking off anxiety. Arguably the disciple most distressed by Jesus' arrest and crucifixion (besides Judas Iscariot), Peter writes from the experience of anguish, remorse, and self-contempt. Peter could have wallowed in shame and regret for his whole life and been conquered by it (in fact, Jesus told him that's what the devil intended for him), but Peter conquered his anxiety. Can you imagine the distress he experienced in the garden, the courtyard, the upper room, and the sea? Look how Jesus changed him! Peter later writes his readers,

"Humble yourselves, therefore, under God's mighty hand, that he may lift you up in due time. Cast all your anxiety on him because he cares for you. Be alert and of sober mind. Your enemy the devil

prowls around like a roaring lion looking for someone to devour. Resist him, standing firm in the faith, because you know that the family of believers throughout the world is undergoing the same kind of sufferings. And the God of all grace, who called you to his eternal glory in Christ, after you have suffered a little while, will himself restore you and make you strong, firm and steadfast. To him be the power for ever and ever. Amen" (1 Peter 5:6-11).

Peter gives us five directives for addressing our anxiety:

1) "humble yourself"—has the idea of ranking yourself lower than others; this makes sense since God promises to exalt you at the right time. It rings of Jesus' words, "servant of all." God's kingdom operates contrary to human logic; the way up is the way down. We are anxious because we're worried about how to go higher in rank, not lower. We're also too proud to admit we have an anxiety problem. "Humble yourself" is a command imperative in Greek, communicating urgency and necessity.

2) "cast off"—*melei* in Greek, literally means to throw something off onto another person. God wants us to throw our anxiety on him. We can trust him to carry the load because he cares for us. *Melei* is the same word used in Mark 4:38 when the boat is filling with water, and the disciples wake Jesus in a panic: "Don't you care if we drown?" Yes, he cares. He cares enough to stay in the boat with them. He cares enough to respond to their question without feeling insulted. He cares enough to save them. That's why we can trust him.

3) "be alert"—be watchful and vigilant, like a sentry in enemy territory. Expect an attack and watch for it.
4) "be of sober spirit"—be even-tempered, self-controlled, circumspect. The idea is that you can calmly handle crises without losing your perspective. You're already on a 360-watch; nobody can sneak up on you, so you are not sidelined by any activity. This might be our biggest snare in ministry: we don't see the enemy coming (not circumspect), or we think everyone is the enemy (not dispassionate). Why we react poorly, why we panic, why we lay awake night after night.
5) "resist the devil"—the concept is intentional opposition, bracing yourself to defend, planting your feet so he can't knock you over. Ephesians 6 tells us how. After the list of critical pieces for warfare, Paul ends with the most important ones: the Sword of the Spirit, which is the word of God (Timothy calls it a two-edged sword in 2 Timothy 2:15), and praying in the Spirit on all occasions. Resisting the devil is futile without the Holy Spirit. It doesn't matter how many leadership podcasts you listen to, how many management books you've read, how popular you are in your church. You cannot resist the devil apart from the filling power of the Holy Spirit.
6) "stand firm in the faith"—Paul says, "Put on the full armor of God so that you can take your stand against the devil's schemes" (Ephesians 6:11). A soldier has on a breastplate, and he's holding a shield—both are in front of him. He is

facing the enemy's attack, and therefore, he is watching and ready. We can't stand firm if our backs are turned. But we take a stand, knowing that the devil will try to trick us. He's the Deceiver, the Father of Lies. So he's coming at us when we're not circumspect. He's attacking our minds and telling us to ignore the signs of stress.

We can't skip the roaring lion part. That preaches. The devil prowls like a roaring lion; again, he represents a distorted imitation of God, the Lion of Judah, who inspires awe and respect in some 150 places in Scripture. The devil is a prowling lion.

WATCHING THE LIONS

Did you ever take your kids to the zoo? Our boys couldn't wait to see the lions. Usually, the lions profoundly disappointed us because they were nearly always asleep. Male lions sleep 18-20 hours per day.

With the exclusion of mating, lions get up to do two things: hunt and eat.

First, the hunt. Lions do not hunt alone. They work together, coming at their prey from all angles. A wildebeest or water buffalo would need 360 vision to anticipate all the ways in which it will be stalked and attacked by lions. Even at 500 pounds, an African lion can run up to 50 mph for short periods. From a stand-still position, it can cover 36 feet in a single jump in a fraction of a second. A lion's eyesight is eight times better at night than a human's. Before you even realize that a lion is in your vicinity, you're dead.

Second, the roar. When a lion roars, it's authoritative and dominating. Lions roar to warn other lions about territory lines and to confuse predators about the number of lions in the pride. They roar after they've killed their prey. A lion's roar can reach the same decibels as a plane taking off. Their roar can be heard for a five mile radius! A lion's roar is terrifying.

Although the zoo was our normal jam, once we took our boys to a safari park in the mountains of Virginia. At the park, African animals roamed in large, penned areas, surrounded by Jurassic Park-style electrified fences, at least 20 feet high. We were pumped to see the lions.

As we were walking along the paved walkways toward the lion area, a tractor pulled toward us, hauling trailers heaped with huge racks of raw animal ribs. It was Carnivore Day at the safari park. We placed ourselves in front of the lion pen. This was going to be awesome for the boys!

Behind the fence, the biggest male paced alone, close to the fence, while the other males and females hung back. The safari keepers climbed up on the trailers, holding huge metal meat hooks in their gloved hands. The lion's golden eyes never left the keeper standing on the trailer while he paced back and forth. Then the keeper tasked with feeding the lions snagged a rib cage with the hook, and with deftness and strength, he hurled the carcass through the air, up over the fence.

The lion leaped toward it—probably ten or twelve vertical feet—his brown mane floating behind his huge, square head, his massive jaws open. He snatched the meat mid-air and landed with it still in his mouth. He violently ripped up the red meat, blood pouring between his teeth and staining his fur.

I (Sue) gasped and covered my littlest boy's eyes. I was not prepared for the trauma of watching a lion eat.

Did you know that a lion's teeth are for tearing and shredding, not for chewing? Peter uses the Greek word *katapinō*, meaning "devour" to describe how the devil, as a roaring lion, intends to eat us. *Katapinō* means to grind into liquid and drink. The process turns red meat into blood, which the lion gulps down.[10]

The devil does not intend to play with you like a housecat with a mouse. He intends to shred and liquefy you. Drink and swallow you. Immediately.

If this scenario is true for every believer, think how seriously the devil wants to devour us pastors and ministry leaders. We are carcasses to him. This is why we experience suffering. The writer of Hebrews instructs, "Have confidence in your leaders and submit to their authority, because they keep watch over you as those who must give an account. Do this so that their work will be a joy, not a burden, for that would be of no benefit to you" (Hebrews 13:17). If the devil can devour pastors, who will shepherd the flock?

THE PIT OF DEPRESSION

Lifeway Research reports that between 18 and 23% of pastors struggle with mental health issues.[11] Most likely, the statistic is

---

[10] Katapino, G2666, 1 Peter 5:8, *Blue Letter Bible*, https://www.blueletterbible.org/lexicon/g2666/niv/mgnt/0-1/

[11] Marty Duren, *Lifeway Research*, 22 August 2022, https://research.lifeway.com/2022/08/22/dealing-with-depression-when-youre-the-pastor

higher, since the Church hesitates to talk honestly and compassionately about mental health. Pastors are not weak or pessimistic. We are engaged in a battle for our spiritual, physical, mental, and emotional survival. The enemy is attempting to gulp us down.

Depression can be a symptom of trauma, disappointment, chemical imbalance, or mental illness. If you struggle with depression, you are not alone. Individuals are unique, and their struggle for mental health is equally unique. Every body uniquely self-protects and shuts down to mitigate chaos and pain. Please do not overlook or dismiss chronic sadness, anxiety, grief, or depression. Your body is signaling you for more caregiving. Find a counselor and/or doctor and treat your depression and anxiety.

Chronic depression and grief are not spiritual deficiencies; church rhetoric is not the answer. C. S. Lewis spoke about cliché Christian responses to grief and depression in *A Grief Observed*: "Talk to me about the truth of religion and I'll listen gladly. Talk to me about the duty of religion and I'll listen submissively. But don't come talking to me about the consolations of religion or I shall suspect that you don't understand."[12]

You don't understand what you don't understand. Talk to someone who does.

THE GRIP OF GRIEF

Grief is equally complex. We have spent decades of our lives sifting through grief and grief recovery. That's us being honest, not walking around crying all the time.

---

12 C. S. Lewis, *A Grief Observed*, Harper One, 2015, 25. (originally published by Faber and Faber, 1961 under the pseudonym N. W. Clerk).

Grief does not mean you're always sad. It does mean you exist while managing overwhelming emotions of despair. "Grief, simply stated, is an amputation." Some normal part of your life (like a leg) no longer exists, yet your brain keeps sending messages to your body about what it's doing and how it feels. The thinking part of your brain feels your leg and feels the "phantom pain" of an amputee. Your leg is not coming back, and you know it. You just can't wrap your head around walking without it.

We will all experience pain in our personal lives. Perhaps your child engages in self-harm. A friend ghosts you (which also means leaving your church). You have continual conflict with a sibling, so you stop speaking. Your health vanishes. Your parent dies. Your business bankrupts. Your spouse betrays you. Your career ends. The list goes on. We have all experienced pain on a personal level. Our experiences differ, but pain is pain.

Grieving is not a condemnation of faith. It's the opposite. Jesus, the Man of Sorrows, grieved over Lazarus, over Jerusalem, over a sinful world. Laments fill the Bible, especially in the Old Testament. David, Solomon, and most of the major and minor prophets wrote laments. The danger of grief lies not in facing pain and sadness but in hunkering down with it. Grief remains entrenched in the past, but hope trusts in the future.

Pastor and licensed therapist Karen Blandino talks about the power of recognizing "intangible grief," a term that has grown in use since 2020. Intangible grief refers to loss without a definitive cause. In the past few years, we can probably all point to a number of factors, but no single fixable factor that has generated such a profound sense of loss and longing in our hearts. We have personally experienced a succession of heartbreaks, traumas, and decisions that have left us with intangible grief, personally and corporately.

Anyone who experiences deep loss often recognizes the cavity in another person who's experiencing grief. The reason for the loss is irrelevant; the body doesn't recognize the difference or the severity of grief. Grief is grief. We who have grieved deeply can see the vacancies in someone's eyes and understand the dislocated connections in their sentences. When we feel compassion and empathy for others, we tap into the character of God.

> Grief is grief.

Jesus feels compassion for us. That's why he let himself suffer, why he chose a horrific death over a quick one. He leaned into the agony of loss, rejection, and shame so that no person would ever have to walk through that valley alone. Jesus declares this mission in Galilee during his first at-bat in Nazareth. He's asked to read before his home crowd, and Jesus boldly chooses to read Isaiah 61. Look at the first three verses from Jesus' perspective, from the Man of Sorrows (before anyone saw him grieve):

"The Spirit of the Sovereign Lord is on me, because the Lord has anointed me to proclaim good news to the

> *poor. He has sent me to bind up the brokenhearted, to proclaim freedom for the captives and release from darkness for the prisoners, to proclaim the year of the Lord's favor and the day of vengeance of our God, to comfort all who mourn, and provide for those who grieve in Zion—to bestow on them a crown of beauty instead of ashes, the oil of joy instead of mourning, and a garment of praise instead of a spirit of despair. They will be called oaks of righteousness, a planting of the Lord for the display of his splendor."*

Jesus came to heal us—our hearts, our souls, our minds, our bodies. He promises to grow us into mighty oaks of righteousness. But it's our suffering and pain that will bring him glory. His splendor shines through healing.

When Jesus read from Isaiah, his home crowd didn't cheer for him. They didn't understand the depth of their own loss or their need for saving. They felt threatened by Jesus' authority, and they tried to push him off a nearby cliff.

A COMMUNITY OF GRIEF

In 2016, a month after my (Sue's) mother died from a decade-long battle with dementia, I wrote to my website audience about grief. I discovered that I was not alone in my emotions:

> *"All of our experiences are different, yet we all feel the same. I know that's true because I've been reading your comments. You've been thanking me for writing*

about grief because you're tired of feeling alone in yours. Sometimes you private message me or send an email because your grief is so raw you must express it, but you're not ready for others to read it. I understand. (You have no idea what I'm not writing here!) I extend my hands to you, and you extend yours to me, and we will pray for one another. We will pray for the sadness to end because we're human and that's the way we think. (Make it stop!) But we will also pray for endurance through the sadness because we're spiritual beings, and we know grief doesn't just stop. (Make me stronger. Make me kinder. Make me gentler.) Admitting our sadness in no way reflects on the level of our faith. I am sad, but my faith is still strong. (It's my heart that's breaking.) My faith is strong enough to question God without questioning who he is."[13]

That's what I wrote then. That I would not question God's character. But here's the thing. When enough losses happen—when the grief compounds and we haven't armed ourselves for more attacks from all the blind spots around us—we will question God's character. We will make assumptions, assign judgment, and grow bitter or depressed. We have to stay vigilant. We have to keep our eyes on the predator.

Our way back to faith requires an authentic discovery of God's character. Even Job, who never learned the catalyst for his

---

[13] Sue Schlesman, "Grief sucks," Sueschlesman.com, Sueschlesman.com/grief-sucks, 22 August 2016.

suffering, told God, "I know that you can do all things; no purpose of yours can be thwarted. . . . Surely I spoke of things I did not understand, things too wonderful for me to know. . . . My ears had heard of you, but now my eyes have seen you'" (Job 42:1-6).

HEALTHY HEARTBEATS FOR "A BOTTOMLESS PIT":

1) Read *On Grief and Grieving* by David Kessler and Elisabeth Kubler-Ross, *Forgiving What You Can't Forget* by Lysa TerKeurst, and/or *Get Out of That Pit* by Beth Moore.

2) See a grief therapist. Look into EMDR, a therapy developed for overriding your sympathetic nervous system so you can process your loss and implement recovery.

3) Start a thankfulness journal. Every day, write down at least three things you're thankful for in a journal or in your phone notes.

4) Listen to the Brittany Jones interview on *Stress Test* Podcast, "Break the Stigma: A Pastor's Journey with Mental Health," Episode 11, 21 Sept. 2023.

PART 2:

A NEW WAY TO WORK
(The Hope for Stress)

"Then Jesus said, 'Come to me, all of you who are weary and carry heavy burdens, and I will give you rest. Take my yoke upon you. Let me teach you, because I am humble and gentle at heart, and you will find rest for your souls. For my yoke is easy to bear, and the burden I give you is light.'"

—Matthew 11:28-30

CHAPTER 6:
A MESSAGE FOR THE HEAVY-HEARTED

"Come to me, all of you who are weary and carry heavy burdens, and I will give you rest."
—Matthew 11:28

What a nice concept. You've probably seen this framed or cross-stitched on a pillow. We all want rest, yet somehow we never get enough of it.

When we were young in the ministry, we assumed Jesus' directive in Matthew 11 was for sad, lonely people. We quoted it at funerals. We shared it with parents of wayward children.

But we must probe deeper. The context of Jesus' invitation doesn't line up with last-ditch platitudes. When Jesus teaches these encouraging words, he has already delivered some harsh warnings to his disciples about the cost of following him. Before promising to heal heavy hearts, he told his followers to expect hardship.

PULL BACK THE CURTAIN

I (Shane) remember my early days of pastoral ministry being filled with ecstasy and hope. I was no longer working on a sales floor. No more misogyny and obscene language from my colleagues. All Jesus work.

In church world, we opened in prayer, met people's needs, and reached our city with the gospel. Our work environment played Christian music through the sound system. Crosses decorated the walls. My parenting was celebrated if I left work early to get my kids off the bus.

Every day, I thought, *I can't believe I get paid to do this!* I still think that. Even when I'm having a horribly hard day filled with difficult meetings, I think, *I can't believe I get to advance the kingdom today.* This is the beauty and wonder of ministry. Many days and countless moments have been filled with those thoughts.

But let's be honest, there are many heavy-hearted moments in ministry, too. If you've been in ministry for any length of time, you've thought, "I can't do this anymore" or "I didn't sign up for this." A few years into each of my ministry jobs, someone or something pulled back the curtain, revealing the great and terrible Oz. I saw regular people pulling levers and pretending they could keep the Christian show going. I saw my own inadequacies as clear as day, and everyone else saw them, too.

All churches (staff and congregations) are filled with normal, flawed humans struggling to obey God. Nobody's growing perfectly, ever. Whether we're paid staff or volunteers, at some point, we see that we've put some people on pedestals, and they're not so remarkable after all. The people we've admired are sometimes angry, discouraged, snippy, vain, or insecure. They don't take suggestions well or don't apologize when they've failed in their responsibilities. They're broken.

> All churches (staff and congregations) are filled with normal, flawed humans struggling to obey God. Nobody's growing perfectly, ever.

Our ministry expectations can morph into disappointment. Pastoring is too hard. We find that the people-business and the soul-business are rife with conflicts. We realize that we're a lot more broken than we thought.

We will struggle to lead if we serve with heavy-laden hearts. If we take ownership of work that isn't ours, we will feel discouraged, disillusioned, or betrayed. Maybe we even feel shame or guilt because we don't like how we feel about ministry and church. We expected better.

Although Jesus ached for the world, he didn't work with a heavy-laden heart. He felt compassion, not anxiety, for the lost.

His soul rested. How did he manage this? (You know, besides being perfect.)

JESUS WAS NOT A WORKAHOLIC

When we read about Jesus and his ministry, we're struck by the 24/7 nature of his life. Jesus accomplished more in 3½ years than we could in decades of ministry.

We assume Jesus was a workaholic, right? He was perfect, so he must have perfected the 60- or 80-hour workweek. He rose early and ministered late. He welcomed masses of people who were diseased, deranged, and despairing. He empathized and touched them. He spoke to people individually, followed them to their homes, and ate meals with them. He was so tired he could fall asleep in a boat rolling on stormy seas.

How did Jesus do it? How did he work so hard, accomplish so much, and yet see individuals for who they were? How could he speak to thousands and still notice those hiding in the shadows—people like Bartimaeus, Zacchaeus, and the woman with the issue of blood? How could Jesus condemn the self-righteousness of the Pharisees and simultaneously forgive the adulterous woman?

Jesus' work was entirely marked by a relational approach; even while he carried the mission of saving the world squarely on his shoulders, he stopped for the one. He preached to big crowds (we all love that), yet he tucked inside every big sermon a particular application for the men and women on his leadership development track. His messages contained application for the critics, the questioning, and the convinced. He confronted his enemies with the reality of their lies and misunderstandings, yet he welcomed inquiries from seekers without shaming them for their confusion.

As pastors, we carry the weight of organized ministry with our compassion for the marginalized, the grieving, and the oppressed. We make time for the church members who interrupt our conversations, show up at our doors, and leave us a dozen bizarre emails about how we could preach better. Harder yet, we find compassion and wisdom for the people who oppose every agenda or idea we have.

Jesus was too holy to be a workaholic. Workaholism is the idolatry of production, not perfectionism. Jesus never worshiped anything—not even his calling, one of the devil's temptations in the wilderness. Jesus remained fully committed to the will of his Father and his identity as the Son. Work for Jesus was an act of love and obedience, a gift to the people around him and submission his Father's will.

LIVING OUT THE GIFT OF WORK

We tend to work for the mission we want to accomplish rather than working to let God accomplish his mission. Proverbs 4:23 (NLT) says, "Guard your heart above all else, because it determines the course of your life." You must figure out what you crave because that determines your decisions and direction.

In Matthew 10 and 11, Jesus explains to his disciples why and how to work.

First, Jesus drops several bombs on them. He has a different approach to leadership development—uncover the obstacles first because motivation and expectation reveal the heart condition. He makes it easy for them to say "no." Their responses unmask their hearts.

Jesus gave his disciples these confusing and complex directives:

- » Heal the sick, drive out demons, raise the dead, cure leprosy—are you kidding me?
- » Don't take any money with you—what?
- » Curse those who won't listen—uh-oh
- » Be shrewd because you are sheep, living among wolves—now I'm really nervous
- » Expect persecution (arrests, indictments, flogging)—ah, no thanks
- » Everyone will betray you and hate you—even my family?
- » You will endure what I endure—why won't you protect me?
- » God will acknowledge you if you acknowledge him and vice versa—can you elaborate?
- » I have not come to bring peace but a sword—now I'm confused; that doesn't seem like you
- » You must lose your life to find it—huh?
- » You will be rewarded for the deeds done in my name—gee, thanks, but I'm too scared to do anything!

Then Jesus takes his followers along the Galilean coastline, town by town. While they walk together, Jesus hears that his cousin John has been imprisoned by Herod. Jesus utilizes the crisis to illustrate what he has just taught his disciples: ministry is going to be hard. You will suffer, and anyone who rejects Jesus' message will also suffer.

Then, in full view of the little towns of Korazin, Bethsaida, and Capernaum, where Jesus did countless miracles, Jesus curses them for their unbelief. (They are still uninhabited today.)

Jesus praises the innocence of his listeners, who are probably in massive freak-out mode by now. Jesus reminds them that he is God the Son, who obeys the will of God the Father:

> "*At that time Jesus said, 'I praise you, Father, Lord of heaven and earth, because you have hidden these things from the wise and learned, and revealed them to little children. Yes, Father, for this is what you were pleased to do. All things have been committed to me by my Father. No one knows the Son except the Father, and no one knows the Father except the Son and those to whom the Son chooses to reveal him'" (Matthew 11:25-27).*

In other words, Jesus intimately knows his Father. Jesus' work is commissioned by his Father. And Jesus chooses those who want to know his Father. Jesus gives his disciples hope, and then he calls them in verses 28-30.

> *Come follow me. Do what I'm doing. Stop worrying about the outcome. (That's my responsibility.) Trust me. I will make you into the greatest version of yourself, the version I imagined since the foundation of the world.*

DOES JESUS UNDERSTAND MY BURDENS, REALLY?

Let's consider the condition of the people Jesus called to come to him and with him. They are "weary and burdened." The word *weary* in Greek is a verb meaning "to grow fatigued, tired, or exhausted." The aorist tense has the idea of something happening in the past but with continual effect. *Burdened* is another verb, sometimes translated in English as *heavy-laden*, reflecting the concept of placing a burden on someone or something. Both have the idea of carrying an overly heavy load, like a pack donkey with too many bundles. But the subject is the receiver of the action, not the doer.

That's us. We over-burden ourselves to accomplish more, achieve more, become more, and we're not even supposed to be carrying the load. Jesus says, "Come, follow me, and I will make you fishers of men" (Matthew 4:19). God will take the calling you have wanted to do—maybe something you are already doing—and he says he will transform that gift into something bigger than you could ever imagine. He just needs your heart.

How remarkable that Jesus calls the weary and burdened individuals to himself instead of calling the organized, refined, and successful people! Jesus walks the dusty roads, surrounded by the poor, diseased, and marginalized. He chooses ordinary men, fishermen, tax collectors, Zealots, and women released from demons to be his mentees, his unpaid staff. He calls them to leave their businesses and bring nothing along. He calls them to restful work.

Even the rich and educated followed Jesus, and some willingly put their fortunes and reputations on the line. The synagogue leader Jairus, desperate for his daughter's life, believes in Jesus' power enough to guide him through crowded streets to his home (he also built the temple in Capernaum). Nicodemus and Joseph of Arimathea risk their lives and fortunes to bury Jesus, an executed criminal.

We can find freedom in the reckless love that Jesus models. He calls us to join him on his mission, not from the pinnacle of our success but in the midst of our desperation.

> We can find freedom in the reckless love that Jesus models.

If we humbly bring him our heavy burdens, we are able to consider inlisting the help of doctors, counselors, mentors, and family. Jesus calls us to come to him first. He wants us to know that he is the destination for healthy rest. Not an improved schedule or healthy alternatives or therapy alone. Jesus is the first and most promising place to bring our burdens.

THE QUALITY OF WORK
None of us have a light burden in the ministry. That's why we go to conferences, listen to podcasts, and read books. We want to get better at managing the load. We want success in ministry. We want to complete our mission—to carry the load to completion.

Remember the context of Jesus' words. He instructed us to find rest in our work, not in spite of our work. Matthew scholar Frederick Dale Bruner reminds us that the center of Jesus' call to rest is a toll for labor:

> *"Jesus realizes that the greatest gift he could give the tired is a new way to carry life, a fresh way to bear responsibilities. . . . Jesus offers equipment. Jesus means that obedience to his Sermon on the Mount [his yoke] will develop in us a balance. . . . An easy life is a myth."*[14]

Days after Jesus imparts his wisdom concerning suffering, John is beheaded, and Jesus attempts to find space to grieve. The crowds follow him, so he agrees to teach them by the sea. Their provisions run out, and Jesus performs a miraculous feeding. He sends his disciples across the sea, and he retreats to pray. From the mountaintop, Jesus can see the disciples straining against a storm, so he walks on the water and calms the storm. When they arrive at Gennesaret, throngs of people meet him with their sick and diseased, and he heals them.

Jesus has prioritized the crowds for days. Non-stop. Even his attempts at rest seem interrupted.

But Jesus never hurries.

THE QUALITY OF REST

In Matthew 11:28, Jesus promises, "I will give you rest." The Greek word for *rest* in this verse is *anapaou*, meaning "to cease from any movement or labor; to give rest or take rest; to refresh; to be

---
[14] Frederick Dale Bruner, *Matthew: A Commentary, Vol. 1: The Cristbook, Matthew 1-12*, Eerdmans 2004, 538.

calm in a patient expectation."[15] That makes sense. That's what we think rest means. Jesus uses the same word when he invites the disciples to come away to a quiet place with him. *Anapaou* is the same Greek word Jesus uses in the Garden of Gethsemane when he asks his disciples, "Are you still sleeping and resting? Enough. The hour has come" (Mark 9:31). In the garden, Jesus' disciples are zonked out. They're not thinking about the betrayal and death Jesus had revealed to them just hours before.

A stone's throw away, Jesus is praying in agony, sweating blood, because he understands that the pinnacle of his purpose will commence shortly. He will endure the cross, alone and rejected.

We shake our heads in judgment when we see the disciples sleeping. We believe they're self-absorbed, unaware idiots to be sleeping during a time like this. Jesus had already indicated that Judas would betray him, and then Judas left the upper room.

How are they not understanding what's happening? They are resting at the wrong time.

They're crashing. They are doing what we, in ministry, do when we're finally off the clock. We work until we're too exhausted to pay attention to the spiritual warfare around us.

In a recent conversation with Mark Batterson, he stated, "We should work from rest, not to rest."[16] When we work to get to rest, we operate in the temporal world, in our own strength and weakness; however, when we work from rest, we work in God's strength. God must work in us before he can work through us.

---

15 Anapauo, G373, Matthew 11:28, *Blue Letter Bible*, https://www.blueletterbible.org/lexicon/g373/niv/mgnt/0-1/

16 Mark Batterson, Zoom call, 23 March 2023.

We have to couple Jesus' directive to rest with his promise of rest. He states, "You will find rest for your souls" while you are yoked in work. Whenever Jesus took significant time to rest and pray (Luke 8:23-25, Matthew 14:22-36), he emerged and performed some of his most powerful miracles of healing, provision, and exorcism. When you rest at work with Jesus, your work will be filled with God's power. You find rest for your soul.

RE-EXAMINING REST
We all have logical solutions for resting from work. Which do you use most?

- » Vacations with the family
- » Date nights and vacations with spouse
- » Time off from speaking and leading (share pulpit time, leading meetings, etc.)
- » Scheduling your days/calendar
    - In thirds per day: Eight hours work, eight hours sleep, eight hours family/household/exercise, etc.
    - Planning "margin" or space in your calendar for slowing down, talking with people, not missing moments with your family
    - Five days on, two days off
    - Planning blocks: exercise, devotions, work, family time, sleep, friends/hobbies—set your kids' activities and spouse time first!
- » Intentional friendships
- » Leadership development

- » Soul work: spiritual retreats, prayer days, etc.
- » Evangelism—intentional relationships with lost people
- » Sabbatical
- » Planned time for reflection, growth, rest, and restoration
- » Guilt-free paid time off

All of this seems like a lot of planning just to get healthy, doesn't it?

Yes. Get a rhythm in your calendar, and don't think about planning anymore; just launch your new schedule. Establish rhythms for your life that create rest because you're leading from a place of rest and renewal.

> Establish rhythms for your life that create rest because you're leading from a place of rest and renewal.

WHO'S IN CHARGE HERE?

Stress uncovers our authority issues. Who's in charge of your emotions? Your thoughts? Your responses? Your body processes information from the inside out. Jesus rebuked the Pharisees for their words by saying, "You brood of vipers, how can you who are evil say anything good? For the mouth speaks what the heart is full of" (Matthew 12:34). Your souls—your heart, as the Bible calls it—determines what you believe. What you believe in your heart, you think in your mind. What you think in your mind, you feel in your emotions. What you feel in your emotions, you act out through your behavior.

Whenever you face a crisis, whether it's cancer, rebellious children, a death, or a betrayal, your body emits evidence of your inner faith.

Are you distrustful of God's providence? Out comes doubt, obsession, worry.

Are you triggered by unresolved trauma? Out comes blame, fear, destructive coping.

If you're full of faith, authentic faith-filled praise comes from your mouth and your actions. Only when Jesus operates as the authority of our lives can he give us rest. If we insist on controlling our own rest and recovery—walling ourselves off or drawing lines between the people we trust and the people we don't—then we have assumed authority over our own lives.

That's why we live with debilitating stress.

MAKING JOYFUL FOLLOWERS AND PEACEFUL LEADERS

When Jesus said, "I will give you rest," he wasn't talking about vacation time, although vacations are helpful. Expecting God to eliminate our stress simply because we take a vacation grossly misses the context and the application of this promise.

Jesus promises to give us rest when we come to him.

When we take his yoke upon us (that part is coming up next!)

Our schedules might improve by incorporating helpful laws and lessons. Our vacations might give us a glimpse of peace before return to the grind. But our work won't be different unless we accept Jesus' invitation to carry our loads with him. His work. His way.

HEALTHY HEARTBEATS FOR "A MESSAGE FOR THE HEAVY-HEARTED":

1) Listen to Scott Wilson's interview called "Embracing Sabbatical" on *Stress Test* Podcast, Episode 6, and Mark Batterson's interview called "Three Powerful Words to Lower Your Stress" on *Stress Test* Podcast, Episode 4, June 12, 2023.

2) Read and process *Sacred Rhythms* by Ruth Haley Barton.

3) Read *It's Not Supposed to Be This Way* by Lysa TerKeurst or *Rising Strong* by Brené Brown.

CHAPTER 7:

THE PATHWAY TO PEACE

"Peace I leave with you; my peace I give you. I do not give to you as the world gives. Do not let your hearts be troubled and do not be afraid."
—John 14:27

Even under the weight of pastoral leadership, we pastors cultivate hope that our churches will expand, our people will grow, our staff will develop, our family will thrive. We will get healthier.

Stress blocks your pathway to peace. You've tried all the breathing and walking, but you still can't move forward.

Distress and anxiety are weights too heavy to carry. We grow weary lugging them around. The writer of Hebrews tells us how to rid ourselves of the oppressive emotional, spiritual, and mental weights. Weights that keep us curled up on the couch and prompt us to avoid social gatherings or live in constant panic:

> *"Let us throw off everything that hinders and the sin that so easily entangles. And let us run with perseverance the race marked out for us, fixing our eyes on Jesus, the pioneer and perfecter of faith. For the joy set before him he endured the cross, scorning its shame, and sat down at the right hand of the throne of God. Consider him who endured such opposition from sinners, so that you will not grow weary and lose heart" (Hebrews 12:1-3).*

The Greek word for throw off is *apotethimi*, meaning "to cast aside or push off."[17] Not reschedule. Not add to your "work on this next" list. *Hurl it away* from you. Why? Because the weight of this world *easily entangles* us. This verb phrase embodies the context of a foot race, something the ancient world completely understood. Two runners are jostling for position as they race over the rocky landscape. Entangling is the strategic, intentional action of pushing into another runner, stretching out your legs to trip him and send him crashing to the ground, to put him out of the race.

This is what your stress will do to you. This is what the devil is using your stress to do. He's not sending you warning signals so you will get healthier. He's whispering that *everything's fine. Your stress is temporary; it's a natural pathway toward success. Just work harder and do better. You've got this. You'll get all the weight better distributed as soon as you are able, after the next crisis. You'll shed some pounds, take another vacation, add a date night. Everything will be fine.*

Just carry the weight a little longer.

---

17 Apotithemi, G659, Hebrews 12:1, *Blue Letter Bible*, www.blueletterbible.org/lexicon/g659/niv/mgnt/0-1/

The world and its ruler, the devil, shape us to believe that our ministry successes and failures define who we are, so if we work a little harder or a little longer, we'll bring God the glory and honor he deserves.

> The world and its ruler, the devil, shape us to believe that our ministry successes and failures define who we are, so if we work a little harder or a little longer, we'll bring God the glory and honor he deserves.

It's a lie. You don't have to accomplish anything. Our successes don't bring God glory. Our transformation does. Our brokenness does. Jesus' entire self-declared mission was "to bestow on them a crown of beauty instead of ashes, the oil of joy instead of mourning, and a garment of praise instead of a spirit of despair. They will be called oaks of righteousness, a planting of the Lord for the display of his splendor" (Isaiah 61:3).

God calls us his holy priesthood. His bride. His beloved. When we're being our created selves.

Before we accomplish anything and even when we destroy everything, God calls us the object of his affection in the most radical love story of time. God has created us for eternity in his presence. Paul reminds the Corinthians, "If in this life only we have hope in Christ, we are of all men most miserable" (1 Corinthians 15:19). We were made for more.

Not bigger churches.

Not Christian governments.

Not perfect families.

We were made to be like him, to reflect his glory, and to see him for who he is.

"Yes, dear friends, we are already God's children, right now, and we can't even imagine what it is going to be like later on. But we do know this, that when he comes we will be like him, as a result of seeing him as he really is" (1 John 3:2-3, TLB).

Seeing Jesus for who he is provides us protection from skewed expectations about ministry and purpose. Jesus safeguards us by carrying the weight with us and for us.

DO NOT FALL AWAY

Jesus offered the promise of protection to his disciples as one of his last acts before he died. After a confusing conversation over dinner, a foot-washing, and an alarming prophecy about dying, Jesus tells his disciples, "All this I have told you so that you will not fall away" (John 16:1). Jesus knew that obedience would be hard. That suffering would threaten our faith. And that all of us would want to quit because it seems too hard to trust.

True obedience is an act of faith. When we tell our toddlers to eat their vegetables and brush their teeth, we're asking them to trust our perspective. We know that healthy habits are important, but they don't. They must obey; someday, they'll have a more mature perspective. They'll be able to understand why vegetables and teeth-brushing are important. But until that time comes, they must obey.

Nothing that you ever want to do is obedience; that's preference. Obedience is only required in situations where we don't want to do something.

The disciples experienced more trauma than we can understand. They gave up everything to follow Jesus, and then they had to watch him be arrested, convicted, and executed. Look how Jesus prepared his disciples for their trauma. Jesus tells the eleven that they will be thrown out of their synagogues and killed (nothing could be worse than that) but that all these events are for their good. Ironically, Jesus is the one about to be tortured and killed, but he reassures their fear by saying:

» I understand that you are grieving because of what I'm saying
» I will send you an Advocate, someone who will judge the world for its sin and intercede for you

Jesus gets us. He understands that we don't understand him. He prepares us anyway. He wants us to walk through heavy times because that's how we learn to depend on him and obey him.

If Jesus didn't understand how difficult following him would be, he would never have said, "Take up your cross daily" (Luke 9:23). He gave the disciples and us a deliberate, mind-blowing order. He told us to pick up an instrument of torture and shame, put it on our beaten-up backs, and remind ourselves that the Father loves us. Our calling was not a mistake. God reminds us in Psalm 30:5 that "weeping lasts for the night, but joy comes in the morning."

We are going to weep. But not forever.

There's a pathway to peace, no matter how dark your life looks at the moment. Jesus promised, "Now is your time of grief, but I will see you again and you will rejoice, and no one will take away your joy. In that day you will no longer ask me anything. Very truly I tell you, my Father will give you whatever you ask in my name. Until now you have not asked for anything in my name. Ask and you will receive, and your joy will be complete" (John 16:22-24).

The pathway to peace during suffering and exhaustion leads us toward spiritual, mental, emotional, and physical health. Let's consider the precedent, performance, pattern, pace, and perfection that Jesus left us. He obviously believed that peace and joy followed suffering.

PERFORMANCE OF JESUS

Jesus didn't perform. He measured the rich offerings against the widow, the Pharisee's laws against the spirit of the Sabbath, the outward good deeds against the inside of the heart. Jesus drew comparisons in every story. "You have heard it said . . . but I say to you . . ."

We understand performance reviews. In sales, top producers get financial incentives and rewards based on performance. Bonuses, trips, and accommodations are celebrated in the public space. Early on, salespeople realize one hard truth: it doesn't matter what you did last year. It matters what you're doing now.

Whenever our performance hinges on temporary pleasure, we remained worried about losing something. Eternally-focused performance brings introspection and conviction. David wrote, "Search me, O God, and know my heart; test me and know my anxious thoughts. See if there is any offensive way in me, lead me in the way everlasting" (Psalm 139:23-24). James described the process like this: "Anyone who listens to the word but does not do what it says is like someone who looks at his face in a mirror and, after looking at himself, goes away and immediately forgets what he looks like" (James 1:23-24). Read the Bible and pray. Ask the questions:

- » What am I ignoring?
- » What am I excusing?
- » What am I afraid of?
- » What do I long for?
- » What is God affirming?

His Word will tell us what to change, if we're not too proud or frightened to search it. "All Scripture is God-breathed and is useful for teaching, rebuking, correcting and training in righteousness, so that the servant of God may be thoroughly equipped for every good work" (2 Timothy 3:16-17). If God is in the business of perfecting us, he will certainly not hide the changes that we need to make.

PRECEDENT FROM JESUS

Jesus set a precedent for living better. No other father figure, pastor, leader, tradition, or cultural dynamic exists without some level of expectation. Jesus doesn't operate that way. He is not the typical leader who responds to disappointment, rejection, or betrayal. He loves and accepts and waits.

Jesus' perspective on the kingdom required him (and his disciples) to expect suffering and comfort simultaneously. "I have told you these things, so that in me you may have peace. In this world you will have trouble. But take heart! I have overcome the world" (John 16:33).

Our created purpose and calling straps us to God himself, making us dependent on him for direction and development. It's the safest and most intimate place we could be. We can chafe against this dependence. We can complain about unrealistic vision, impossible rules, or disheartening predicaments, but if we choose to misread God's will as neglect, we will miss the blessing of growth.

Jesus told his disciples about the fine print. He admitted they wouldn't understand what he was saying until much later—grief and trauma work that way—so he kindly asked for their trust.

Jesus calls us to hope: "Now is your time of grief, but I will see you again and you will rejoice, and no one will take away your joy. In that day you will no longer ask me anything. Very truly I tell you, my Father will give you whatever you ask in my name. Until now you have not asked for anything in my name. Ask and you will receive, and your joy will be complete" (John 16:22-24).

KINGDOM FIRST

As pastors and shepherds, we're naturally drawn toward the hurting. We gravitate toward the broken and step in to administer healing. The Beatitudes in Matthew 5 remind us that suffering is integral to the kingdom, and hope is essential. Without hope, suffering is cruel. Compassion fatigue sets in. Shepherding becomes laborious. Criticism draws defensiveness, reaction, and paranoia.

We will always shift our energy and attention toward problem-solving, strategizing, managing, and controlling. We will call it leadership, exchanging our obedience for approval in a temporal kingdom.

PEOPLE FIRST

When the Pharisees attempted to entrap Jesus concerning the laws of Moses, he responded by saying all of Judaic law hung on only two commandments: love the Lord your God with all your heart, soul, and mind, and love your neighbor as yourself (Matthew 22:37-40). Everything Jesus did—and everything we do, even in crisis—should and must point people to God the Father.

That's the precedent. It's really that simple.

Following the pandemic, our church's kingdom focus became simple and forthright: win the lost and disciple them into the church. Every outreach and study that wanted to resume had to answer these two questions:

1) How are you reaching the lost?
2) How are you discipling the found?

When your church loses all its bells and whistles, you are left with two things: the gospel and the move of God.

> **When your church loses all its bells and whistles, you are left with two things: the gospel and the move of God.**

Our church practiced the great commission before the pandemic, but after COVID, we required our staff and volunteers to prioritize two objectives only: preach the kingdom of God, then multiply the kingdom. We felt called to focus on making disciples, not keeping disciples happy.

"People first" means reaching the lost first. Jesus' mission was clear: "I was sent only to the lost sheep of Israel" (Matthew 15:24). Jesus leaves the 99 for the one. The "one" is the lost. All three parables in Luke 15 (lost sheep, lost coin, lost son) clearly delineate the lost thing as being someone out of relationship with the Father. If you view the lost sheep as a Christian who has left the church, you must wrestle with Jesus' declared mission and the Great Commission. Jesus did not apologize for making the lost his priority. He didn't ignore the found; instead, he invited them to join him in his mission to seek and save the lost.

REST FIRST

Jesus practiced self-care. That's obviously the goal of this book. Your body is the temple of the Holy Spirit. Stop abusing it.

Jesus prioritized rest, emotional health, and spiritual nourishment. He regularly went to solitary places to pray. Interesting, right? He was already God, he was crystal-clear about his mission, and yet he regularly communicated with God about his mission.

I (Sue) wrote in *Soulspeak: Praying Change into Unexpected Places*, "Prayer is where we work out what God is doing and what he wants us to do."[18] I've found that praying Scripture is hugely redemptive in my life, especially during the valleys when I'm not sure what to say or if my heart is pure before the Lord. When we speak praise to God about his goodness and mercy, our faith grows stronger.

God doesn't need us to pray. We need it. If your prayer life has become less effective, do a little self-assessment:

- » How long can you pray?
- » How well do you listen for God's perspective?
- » What is your ratio of praise versus request?
- » How many times has God answered your requests? Has he ever failed you even if his answer did not match your request?

PATTERNS OF JESUS

David asked God to search and know his heart. This is an interesting request, considering that God had called him "a man after

---

[18] Sue Schlesman, *Soulspeak: Praying Change into Unexpected Places*, Lighthouse Publishing, 2019, 56-57.

God's own heart" (1 Samuel 13:14). If anyone already knows God's heart, David does, right? David understood the ease with which his soul could misalign from God's priorities. Paul described the restorative process in Romans 12 as "renewing your mind" (Romans 12:1-2). How do you identify the renewal patterns necessary to avert leadership stress? Simple. Trace the lie you're believing back to its source.

You say you're not believing any lies.

(That's a lie right there. We are all deceived.)

A seed of doubt wedges itself into your soul, a seed like God didn't come through, or God doesn't love you as much as other people, or God hasn't answered your prayers. Like Adam and Eve, you can decide that God isn't completely trustworthy. "The heart is deceitful above all things and beyond cure. Who can understand it?" (Jeremiah 17:9).

You often can't cure yourself from believing the enemy's lies during a crisis because in crisis moments, lies make logical sense. *If God loves me, why hasn't he solved my problems? I'm here killing myself for him!*

Here are some lies that we regularly struggle against. See if any of these feel familiar to you:

- » I am not cut out for ministry
- » No one would follow me if they really knew me
- » I am unworthy or unlovable
- » If I just work longer and harder, everything will be okay
- » If my church doesn't grow, I'm a failure

- » I wish God would speak to me; he's not telling me what to do
- » My critics are right about me
- » Everyone is better off without me

PACE OF JESUS

Jesus is the only person in human history who worked for so short a time and accomplished such radical change. Thronged by thousands, Jesus ministered constantly, and yet he stopped for lepers howling in the distance, blind men begging by roadsides, a man hiding in a tree, and a woman reaching out to touch his robe. He stopped to heal, to teach, and to touch. Always moving and yet never rushed.

Jesus taught his disciples to forgive by forgiving. He taught them to share by sharing. He taught them to love by loving. He let them learn through failing. Sure, he could capture a crowd and pitch a vision. He taught on various levels simultaneously. He addressed the barriers of hunger, sound, and accessibility. He developed organizational structures for his proteges and managed revenue streams for his ministry. He planned sabbaticals—or at least retreats—for himself. He nurtured, rebuked, instructed, and warned.

He completed the work he came to do.

Jesus never seemed to hurry. He doesn't hurry now. According to Peter, "God is not slow concerning his promises," like most people think. God is patient, or *longsuffering*, as the King James Version translates the descriptor in 2 Peter 3:9. In the Greek, however, there is no adjective like *longsuffering* in this verse; instead, the subject *God* does the verb *makrothymeo*, which means to *be patient* or *suffer long*.

Patience is an action, not a personality trait. God chooses to suffer, to wait for us to respond, to choose him back. He doesn't rush us. He's willing to wait. He sees the big picture, and it's worth waiting for. It's worth suffering for. When we experience leadership stress, our anxiety arises from anticipation of the outcome, like a dream or a deadline. We can't see God's big picture; we can only see our own. We believe our agendas sit in jeopardy without decisive, logical action.

Hope absolutely depends on "slowness" (patience). Submitting to God's pace requires the abandonment of hurry. John Mark Comer, in his profound book *The Ruthless Elimination of Hurry*, states, ". . . not only is hurry toxic to our emotional health and spiritual lives, it's also symptomatic of much deeper issues of the heart."[19] To fully trust God's promises and to live in healthy rhythms, we must eradicate hurry from our personal, spiritual, and professional lives. We must adopt the pace that Jesus took. You become what you give your attention to.

PERFECTION OF JESUS

Paul tells the Ephesian church: "So Christ himself gave the apostles, the prophets, the evangelists, the pastors and teachers, to equip his people for works of service, so that the body of Christ may be built up until we all reach unity in the faith and in the

---

19 John Mark Comer, *The Ruthless Elimination of Hurry*, Waterbrook, 2013, 56.

knowledge of the Son of God and become mature, attaining to the whole measure of the fullness of Christ" (Ephesians 4:11-13). *Until we all reach unity and become mature.*

Here's the really cool part. *Attaining to the whole measure of the fullness of Christ* is a participial phrase. That means it's an adjective describing the pastors and teachers; the verb *attaining* has the idea of process. Maturity is already happening. The pastors and teachers are already attaining the full measure of Christ. They are in the process of becoming more like him every day as they obediently live out their calling.

That's our hope. That's how we kill the deadly stress we accept with our thoughts and our emotions. That's how we pull the lies of *not-good-enough* and *it's-too-late* from our souls. We grab anxiety by its roots, we declare the patience of a loving God, and we pull hard, every day, knowing that God is already perfecting us. We are conforming into the image of his Son by showing up.

HEALTHY HEARTBEATS FOR "THE PATHWAY TO PEACE":

1) Read *The Ruthless Elimination of Hurry* by John Mark Comer and *Subversive Sabbath* by A. J. Swoboda.

2) Read and process *Emotionally Healthy Spirituality* by Peter Scazzero.

3) Look over the "Tracing Behavior Back to Belief" in the Resources section in the back of the book. Follow the examples and plug in a behavior or emotion you commonly have; trace it back to a core heart belief.

CHAPTER 8:
LEADING IN A YOKE

"Take my yoke upon you. Let me teach you, because I am humble and gentle at heart, and you will find rest for your souls."
—Matthew 11:29

Now we've got to look at the yoke analogy. It's a bit weird for us.

Rest for my soul? Yes. We'll take it.

A yoke? No, thanks. We've got a hard enough yoke already.

Gentle and humble at heart? How is humility connected to working in a yoke? We just need relief. Jesus came to give us the answers.

THE HARNESS FOR FREEDOM

Jesus explains the connection between work and soul rest by using an analogy of oxen yoked together. From a farming and fishing culture, Jesus' disciples—and any eavesdropping audience members of their day—would have understood Jesus' reference. But maybe they'd need his explanation of the analogy as much as we would.

We know that the yoke is a work tool. In ancient times (and in simple rural farming areas around the world today), farmers used a wooden beam called a yoke beam, with two semi-circles called bows attached on the underside. The bows encircled the heads of two oxen, horses, or mules, who were paired together to pull a cart or plow. In the middle of the beam, the yoke contained a space called the staple. It kept the animals in the bows, spaced far enough apart to walk freely but close enough to walk in tandem.

The Romans paired horses together to pull chariots because horses pull faster than any other animal and can handle the chaos of combatants fighting around them. Ancient farmers, however, could not afford horses; they used mules or oxen for plowing their fields. While horses are faster, oxen are stronger than horses and can pull heavier loads for longer periods of time over more difficult terrain.

The combined power of two animals pulling together produces a multiplied power, not added power. One ox can pull between 1,500 to 3,000 pounds of weight by himself. But two oxen can carry 13,000 to 15,000 pounds together. Their partnership carries up to five times the power of working alone.

Yoked oxen are trained to pull together from their youth. Farmers don't just put any two animals in a yoke and start driving them down the field. Each ox has been raised to work. An untrained ox may only be able to carry half its weight, but a trained ox can carry two to three times its weight. The farmer trains oxen to work together, to learn each other's moves, to work as one. The farmer doesn't risk his sowing or his harvest by attaching his oxen to any animal other than the one they've been trained to pull with. Once a farmer finds the right pairing of oxen, he pairs them *for life*. If one of the oxen dies, the other has to be repurposed; it can no longer pull in a yoke.

The symbolism is clear. Jesus commands us to attach ourselves to *him*. To work with him. To pull with him. Only him, forever.

> Jesus commands us to attach ourselves to him. To work with him. To pull with him. Only him, forever.

Jesus' work is easy because he's doing what God told him to do. Our work is easy because we're pulling with him. We're doing what he tells us to do.

Jesus promises us:

"Believe me when I say that I am in the Father and the Father is in me; or at least believe on the evidence of the works themselves. Very truly I tell you, whoever believes in me will do the works I have been doing, and they will do even greater things than these, because I am going to the Father. And I will do whatever you ask in my name, so that the Father may be glorified in the Son" (John 14:12-13).

Because of the resurrection, we are capable of doing greater works than Jesus did because we are pulling under his yoke—with him. Our success has nothing to do with us. Because of Jesus' resurrection, the Holy Spirit resides in us, equipping and empowering us for the ministry. His yoke is our pathway to freedom, not our pathway to success. Paul encouraged Timothy: "All Scripture is God-breathed and is useful for teaching, rebuking, correcting and training in righteousness, so that the servant of God may be thoroughly equipped for every good work" (2 Timothy 3:16-17). Our lives have always been about doing God's work for God's glory, according to God's Word.

You are equipped for the load you're bearing. Don't try to carry it by yourself because it's not your load.

THE YOKE OF HUMILITY

In case Jesus' life and ministry isn't proof enough, Paul reviews it for the church in Philippi:

> *"If you've gotten anything at all out of following Christ, if his love has made any difference in your life, if being in a community of the Spirit means anything to you, if you have a heart, if you care—then do me a favor: Agree with each other, love each other, be deep-spirited friends. Don't push your way to the front; don't sweet-talk your way to the top. Put yourself aside, and help others get ahead. Don't be obsessed with getting your own advantage. Forget yourselves long enough to lend a helping hand" (Philippians 1:1-4, MSG).*

In other words, if you're having conflict at work, at church, at home, or in yourself, notice the signs of stress and the authority you're giving that stress. You may have confused getting ahead with getting along. You've traded God's agenda for your own. And it's not working well for you. Paul asks the pointed, telling question in verse 2—"Are your hearts tender and compassionate?"

Well, no. Our hearts are all twisted into knots. We don't have the bandwidth for tenderness, and we're experiencing compassion fatigue. That means we're doing our work all wrong.

THE HEAVY YOKE OF PERFECTIONISM

Christianity has done a bang-up job shaming us into perfectionism. We call it excellence, but it's not. It's a strategic assault on our formation by God, who has engineered our abilities, talents, inclinations, personality, and passions into a remarkable combination unique to us individually. If we aren't what our other people want or expect us to be, we feel compelled to conform and improve. However, our only responsibility is maturity and completion in Christ—to be in a process of letting God *perfect* us.

We will never reach perfection here. We will never be enough here.

You are enough for God. Cast off those heavy burdens of performance and perfection and walk easily under the yoke Jesus shoulders with you.

I (Sue) am a reforming perfectionist. I can't even say I'm a recovered perfectionist because I'm not recovered yet, and in my flesh, I don't want to be—I like this description about myself. I finish my work. I do it right. I admire and enjoy it. I don't need a lot of fanfare (but some recognition is nice) because I'm my own worst critic and my own best fan. I obviously need reformation.

When leaders are perfectionists, they hold people to a high standard. This can be good or bad, but it's mostly bad. We don't have the maturity to work to a high standard with mercy, grace, and compassion. Our pride always takes over. Frustration follows and always leaves us angry, disillusioned, critical, and judgmental. These qualities don't serve leaders well.

> We don't have the maturity to work to a high standard with mercy, grace, and compassion. Our pride always takes over. Frustration follows and always leaves us angry, disillusioned, critical, and judgmental.

Here are a few signs that you might struggle with perfectionism:
- » You are constantly frustrated or annoyed
- » You give critical feedback easily but give encouragement sparingly
- » You get angry at others' behavior
- » You use venting, gossiping, or angry outbursts to air your frustration

- » You set standards that are possible for you to meet but nearly impossible for anyone else to meet
- » You struggle to delegate or trust others to accomplish something
- » You don't like the way your staff completes the tasks you've assigned them
- » You are chronically dissatisfied with yourself and your accomplishments
- » Close family and friends hesitate to confide in you or confess to you
- » You worry or obsess over decisions you've already made

HOW PERFECTIONISM AFFECTS YOUR CALLING

When I (Sue) was barely four years old, I told my mom after Sunday night service that I wanted to ask Jesus into my heart. I hadn't committed many sins yet. I was a good little girl who truly wanted to please, but I knew I needed Jesus.

We were Independent Fundamental Baptists, so I already knew about hell. I knew all about doing the right things and not doing the wrong things. I desperately wanted to always do the right things, starting with my decision to ask Jesus to save me.

The story of God's love and Jesus' sacrifice had pulled me to God's heart. My father had died about 18 months before my salvation. I wasn't aware of the father hole yet in my heart—the hole of not knowing my dad or hearing enough details about him. At that time, I only remember an intense desire to be good and for everything to be peaceful and safe.

As I grew, I desired to make things right in the world, to do good as well as be good. By second grade, I was walking down the aisle at Bible camp in tears, telling God I would be a missionary. That was the year I also decided to be a writer. I had a fire in my belly about truth and justice. I cried over the poor kids in Africa and Asia. As I grew, I traveled, read voraciously, and memorized Scripture. I developed both a poetic and a prophetic voice. I honed my talents and abilities to use in the church. I modeled myself after the Proverbs 31 woman, checking off her characteristics one by one, trying to be the perfect Christian lady. My spiritual calling seemed clear and attainable.

ENTER CHRISTIAN BIAS

But I struggled with a few roadblocks to fully living out my calling, of working with Jesus in his yoke.

I was a girl. My conservative, albeit lovely, church context did not allow or approve of a woman's prophetic and pastoral leanings. At most, I could teach children and be a deaconess (like my mom did), tucked away in the basement with toddlers or in the tiny church kitchen with the other ladies. Or I could be a single missionary lady (they showed cool slides, but they wore long skirts in hot climates, and their fate of singleness seemed predestined). Or I could be a pastor's wife (being a woman pastor was not an option for me—again, Independent Fundamental

Baptist). I could play piano and smile at people and sit on the front pew in church.

Obviously, the best and least lonely choice was to be a pastor's wife. I did not play the piano, and I did not care for the front row. I had opinions. But I supposed this was the reason for Proverbs 31—to teach me how to be more holy and quiet in my industry. I memorized the chapter and put it into practice.

Of course, my career choice depended on an available man's desire to marry me. Thus went the 1970s and 80s. Being a good girl, I focused on writing and waiting for a suitable pastor-in-training to marry me when I was old enough and, hopefully, not too old. Being a writer/missionary remained Unmarried Option #2.

IMAGE-MAKER

As much as I had learned about being created in God's image and being called according to his purpose, I never assumed anyone's perspective could demean or disguise my image in Christ. Many people affirmed my service in ministry and my gift for writing and teaching (children), but it took decades for me to connect the dots between my writing and my prophetic and pastoral gifting. It didn't occur to me that a Proverbs 31 woman could be more than a quiet devotional writer who sits and smiles from the front row and takes care of her family in the middle of the night. So when I grew up and actually married a pastor and served everywhere in the church (for free, because I was the wife) at our first couple of churches, I was surprised by my high level of frustration with ministry work. At every turn, my vision and energy hit the ceiling of my limited understanding and expectations. Shane and I struggled to work together in ministry because we wriggled under the roles assigned to us rather than responding to the unique stamp of God on each of us. (As a kid from a blended family, Shane also wore a given stereotype from our churchy environments.)

I stuffed myself into the roles I was allowed to have. Good roles. Necessary roles. But roles that, for me, were not my calling. This happens to all of us at some point. We conform, comply, and contest. We have arguments, personality conflicts, power struggles, and confrontations because we're frustrated and confused. When we don't labor under the yoke God has placed on our shoulders, stress builds in our souls.

We're working in a yoke, but we're pulling against our partner's direction. Maybe someone has said something like this, which crushed your calling just a little bit—

"Your spot is on the front row."

"You preach pretty well for a pastor's wife."

"I didn't vote for your husband."

"I passed you in the hallway, and you ignored me."

"You can't work outside the home if you're a pastor's wife."

"If you can speak that well, I'll bet your husband is really good."

However well-intentioned (or not) the comments are, people's expectations can make us doubt that we should be doing ministry at all. We weave all over the road in a yoke that constricts because we are trying desperately to be perfect for everyone.

WHEN YOUR BUSYNESS IS NOT YOUR BUSINESS

I never realized until I had grown in spiritual maturity and eventually gotten counseling that I had been limiting God's use of my life by trying to live up to other people's expectations. No one had consciously forced me to adapt to a role I didn't want; we all were trying to serve Jesus with the lenses we had. Consequently, we placed expectations on other people. And because I am not a rule-breaker, I noted the expectations and fit myself into the boxes created for me.

I didn't try to inhibit my calling. It happened because I didn't know any better. I didn't interpret God's Word like I do today. By attempting to perfectly play the role of Christian woman/pastor's wife, I had generated a lifestyle of self-imposed stress.

Whenever we do not operate within the calling that God has placed on us, we will feel anxiety within ourselves. We will work too hard and sleep too little. We will endure headaches and stomach aches. We will live with chaos in our bodies. Our souls will suffer. We will find fault with others. We will compare, envy, and compete with other men and women who are living out their callings while we wonder why ours is so difficult to achieve.

COMPASSION FATIGUE

Stress in ministry can occur from our unfailing desire to do good. A perfectionist struggles to set boundaries because the work of helping people never reaches completion. People always need more time, more money, more love.

> People always need more time, more money, more love.

We wear ourselves out trying to save people, love people, and help people. Psychologists term this *compassion fatigue*, which differs from *burnout*, a non-relational state of mental exhaustion. *Compassion fatigue* is emotional, mental, and physical exhaustion from prolonged relational care. I'm personally drawn to orphans, poor children, widows, and women empowerment programs because I feel connected to the emotional and physical needs of these people. Because of my personal experiences, I feel relationally connected to isolated, grieving, and marginalized people. I love walking with the mom who's divorcing or the adult who's grieving a parent's death. I feel their pain deeply, and I desire to help them transition to freedom in spite of loss.

Recovery from anything is a long process. Sometimes I don't have the bandwidth for it. Sometimes it hurts too much. The pain from others' experiences can stir up my own pain. I will spiral if I'm carrying my yoke by myself. In order for me to engage in a ministry calling, I must enlist people to help me. As leaders, we must link arms with others to do any kind of ministry, even the ministry we feel most gifted at doing. We are designed to work in a community.

Author, theologian, and professor A. J. Swoboda writes about how stress consumed him during his pastoral calling in his book *A Glorious Dark*: "*Compassion fatigue* is a term coined by scientists describing what happens when we try to care for everything. If we allow it, our compassion can kill us. That frees us to learn a great lesson: that not every need in the world represents the will of God for my life. I can only carry so much. And I can't carry all of God's compassion, only a little slice of it that has been gifted to me."[20]

You are setting yourself up for compassion fatigue if—
» You worry about someone's problem all the time
» You take responsibility for solving someone's problems or facilitating their recovery
» You command your own responsibilities without delegation or help
» You feel hopeless, afraid, and/or powerless
» You experience high stress, sleeplessness, and inattentiveness
» You need substances, like medication or alcohol, to calm down your mind
» You have reduced feelings of empathy or care for everyone and everything

---

20 A. J. Swoboda, *A Glorious Dark*, 49.

Of course, the Bible has already talked about compassion fatigue. Paul directs his readers' attention to the solution for unhealthy stress in Philippians 2 of *The Message*:

> *"Think of yourselves the way Christ Jesus thought of himself. He had equal status with God but didn't think so much of himself that he had to cling to the advantages of that status no matter what. Not at all. When the time came, he set aside the privileges of deity and took on the status of a slave, became human! Having become human, he stayed human. It was an incredibly humbling process. He didn't claim special privileges. Instead, he lived a selfless, obedient life and then died a selfless, obedient death—and the worst kind of death at that—a crucifixion" (Philippians 2:5-8, MSG).*

Jesus humbled himself. He elevated others. He obeyed his calling. This is why he could tell his disciples to "take up your cross daily and follow me." He doesn't ask us to do anything he hasn't done first, but he's letting us do a much easier version. We haven't given up deity to take on human flesh. We haven't felt the weight of the whole world's sins. We haven't ever been rejected by our Heavenly Father.

Only Jesus has endured those things.

HEALTHY HEARTBEATS FOR "LEADING IN A YOKE":

1) Read *The 21 Irrefutable Laws of Leadership* by John Maxwell and *Dare to Lead* by Brené Brown.

2) Take the "Resilience and Avoidance Assessment" in the Resources at the back of the book.

3) List situations or feelings that make you spiral into discouragement, avoidance, or despair; find the lie embedded in them and pray against it.

4) Identify a person in ministry who frustrates or irritates you. Commit to pray for that person. Look for opportunities to help this person develop in their strengths.

CHAPTER 9:
STEWARDS AND OWNERS

"Take my yoke upon you and learn from me."
—Matthew 11:29

My (Shane's) dad had some nice cars when I was growing up. I was rarely, if ever, allowed to drive them. When I was 16, my dad had a 1966 Mustang convertible.

I borrowed it and drove it through town, honking at friends and nodding at people in a too-cool-for-school way, peppered by fans, shouting, "Dude! Awesome car!" and "When did you get that?"

I didn't tell anyone that it was my dad's car and I wasn't allowed to drive it. For a very brief time (while my dad was at work), I owned a 1966 Mustang convertible. I was driving it, after all. I was in charge.

I soaked in the glory. I circled through town as long as I could before taking it home to place it under cover, back in the garage.

As I walked into the house, I heard my bike fall against the driver-side door.

Uh-oh! Reality check: the Mustang wasn't mine. My dad would remind me of that when he got home. I had scratched the Mustang. I had been arrogant, irresponsible, and reckless. I may have driven the car, but it wasn't mine.

Why is this distinction important?

If we attempt ownership of the ministries we manage for God, we carry a weight and responsibility that we were not designed to carry. This creates stress in our minds and bodies. God allows us to become stewards because he knows we can't handle the responsibility of ownership, yet he wants us involved in his mission. We can't live wisely enough, long enough. We can't redeem our own mistakes. We can't save the world or even ourselves. So, God makes all the sacrifices necessary to give us what we so desperately need.

Then he shoulders the yoke, like he shouldered the cross, and he starts walking uphill toward the kingdom of heaven. In his love and mercy, Jesus fits a circle over our necks and lets us walk with him. He keeps us close so we don't stray or fall or stop.

He just says, "Come, follow me. I will make you fishers of men" (Matthew 4:19). Join my yoke instead of the weight you are carrying.

ASSET PROTECTION

Stewardship is not simply taking care of something, like house-sitting or babysitting, although those actions require careful attention and responsibility. Stewardship demands investment and multiplication.

> **Stewardship demands investment and multiplication.**

In Matthew 25:14-30, a landowner goes on a long journey and entrusts his money to three servants of varying abilities. We know this as the Parable of the Talents. We've used it often to preach about serving, giving, and surrender. Perhaps the most fascinating aspect of the story is the relationship of the stewards to each other and their master. Note that the servants do not compete for the owner's approval. They don't compare their endowments or their return on their investments. The master is in control because he owns the money; he has distributed the talents as he desires. The servants must simply invest the money (translated *talents* in the KJV and *bags of gold* in the NIV). When the owner returns, he wants to see growth.

All three servants—even the one who disobeys the instructions—concern themselves exclusively with pleasing their master, as they understand his character. The servants with five and two talents both invest their allotments and double their money. Their master praises them and gives them the same amount again. We like preaching this sowing and reaping principle because "From everyone who has been given much, much will be demanded; and from the one who has been entrusted with much, much more will be asked" (Luke 12:48). We pastors compare ourselves to the first two servants.

(But often, we are the third. We preserve what God's given us because we're afraid.)

When the master returns and takes an accounting of his investments, he finds out that the third servant has buried the gold in the ground. The master calls him *wicked and lazy* only after the servant has failed. It's unlikely that a good master would entrust one talent (a measure of weight amounting to 75 pounds of silver or gold) to a known sluggard. The servant proves himself lazy when he stops stewarding the master's money like the master told him to. The servant explains himself with this excuse: "'Master,' he said, 'I knew that you are a hard man, harvesting where you have not sown and gathering where you have not scattered seed. So I was afraid and went out and hid your gold in the ground. See, here is what belongs to you.'" In other words, the servant fails because he's afraid of failure; he hides the talent.

Understanding ownership and stewardship is integral to stress management. If you own your ministry—if everything succeeds or fails on your productivity—you also own all of the stress that goes with it. God does not intend for you to own the weight of your ministry. It's not yours.

GOING TO WORK WITH DAD

When our three boys were still preschool age, I (Shane) took all of them to work with me. Sue dressed them like me; they carried little backpacks with books and papers in them; they brought lunch. They sat in my office or rode with me in my car and enjoyed the day. Not once did they feel any stress. They didn't have any assignments at my work other than following me around and behaving. Why? Because they were not responsible for being successful with their day. They just enjoyed spending time with me, their dad, doing what I was doing.

What would it look like for you to join your Heavenly Father at work and let him carry the weight? Could you enjoy the intimacy of being with Jesus every day and not accomplish anything on your own?

HOW TO STEWARD PEACE

Since we are God's stewards, who are called to a life of peace, it must be possible to work and rest simultaneously. How do we steward a peaceful work ethic? Consider allowing these five words to help guide you.

1) Connect. You are called to work under a yoke in a partnership with the King of Kings. Do not allow your boards, your congregation, or even your family to influence you more than Jesus. Pull with him and for him.
2) Calm. You are designed to rest. Your physiology requires you to shut down regularly, not just when you crash from overwork or when you take a vacation. If you won't rest,

won't take a Sabbath each week, or can't sleep at night, your body will have a mental, physical, and spiritual breakdown.

3) Center. Don't confuse the mission with legacy. We are not called to build successful mega-churches or schools or governments or arts programs or non-profits. We are called to spread the gospel and disciple believers. The harvest (i.e., the churches, schools, etc.) belongs to God to grow or prune as he sees fit. Notice what Jesus said prior to explaining the yoke: "All things have been committed to me by my Father. No one knows the Son except the Father, and no one knows the Father except the Son and those to whom the Son chooses to reveal him" (Matthew 11:27). None of our ministry belongs to us.

4) Conserve. Manage your soul, not just your schedule. Listen to your heart. When your stomach tightens in fear, respond by addressing the growing anxiety rather than pushing yourself toward accomplishment. When you're exhausted, sleep; don't try to check off duties "so you can sleep." Train yourself to sleep with an unfinished list. God's work will be completed in his perfect time, at his perfect pace.

5) Cover. Enlist an army of prayer warriors to fight for you and for the ministry. During a particularly difficult culture struggle within our church, we invited a group of people who were powerful in the Holy Spirit and trustworthy to keep confidentiality to pray specifically for our needs. We were honest about our pain. We opened a text thread to

facilitate our specific requests and bring awareness of the spiritual warfare against us. Our prayer group responded with prayers, prophetic words, visions, Scripture, and encouragement. Although we had consistent emails and comments from congregants who said, "We're praying for you, Pastor," having this specific, informed group pray for us bolstered our faith and courage in a unique way.

We all want to please God. But we also want to satisfy our own expectations. We will not set healthy boundaries with people, tasks, or time unless we relinquish control.

THE ISSUE OF RESPONSIBILITY

Your responsibility is relative to your call. Jesus said the master in the story gave different amounts to different servants. He gave "to each according to his own ability" (Matthew 25:15). The master knows what each servant is capable of accomplishing. Our responsibility is relative, but our value is not. When the master returns, he praises and rewards the first two servants equally. They both double their value. He only expresses anger at the third servant for not utilizing the gift he was given.

We cannot play the comparison game with other pastors, leaders, or ministers. God has created each of us for a specific purpose, which means he gifts each of us with specific gifts to accomplish that purpose. The best way to knock out comparison is to pray for other pastors and celebrate their successes. Also, do not let people compare you to others and hold you to the accomplishments that someone else achieves. We are not competing against other pastors or ministries; we are engaged in a war against the devil. As a distraction from God's mission, comparison and competition create enormous stress and insecurity.

REWARD

This story of the stewards ends on a serious note:

> *"Then the servant with the one bag of silver came and said, 'Master, I knew you were a harsh man, harvesting crops you didn't plant and gathering crops you didn't cultivate. I was afraid I would lose your money, so I hid it in the earth. Look, here is your money back.' But the master replied, 'You wicked and lazy servant! If you knew I harvested crops I didn't plant and gathered crops I didn't cultivate, why didn't you deposit my money in the bank? At least I could have gotten some interest on it.' Then he ordered, 'Take the money from this servant, and give it to the one with the ten bags of silver. To those who use well what they are given, even more will be given, and they will have an abundance. But from those who do nothing, even what little they have will be taken away. Now throw this useless servant into outer darkness, where there will be weeping and gnashing of teeth'"* (Matthew 25:24-30).

> The gifts that God has entrusted to you are not yours to use or lose.

The gifts that God has entrusted to you are not yours to use or lose. They are gifts to *steward*. *Using* implies consumerism, which seriously reeks of the Western Church and not the Kingdom of God. Let's pick apart the conclusion of this story just to make sure we understand the implications of stewardship.

- » The master calls the servant "wicked and lazy" for not investing the talent. The guy maintained his ministry—he kept things going. He doesn't even lose any money, yet the master is still angry with him.
- » The master is bold. He is willing to do anything to multiply his wealth. He welcomes the risk. The servant knows this and is intimidated by it because the risk is outside of the servant's control.
- » The master takes away the talent and gives it to the most productive servant. He always rewards obedience.
- » The master turns the wicked servant over to be tortured. The reference to "weeping and gnashing of teeth" reminds us of hell; it would have reminded Jesus' listeners of the same thing. The servant has failed to complete his mission; perhaps he never believed in the mission at all.

God takes stewardship seriously.

HEALTHY HEARTBEATS
FOR "STEWARDS AND OWNERS":

1) Analyze your stress-inducing responsibilities. Is it possible that you've taken ownership of your success? Put your responsibilities on the altar; give control back to God. Which of your responsibilities or stressors can you entrust someone else to manage for you? Choose to give others the freedom to steward an area for God's approval, not yours.

2) Watch Dave Ramsey's conference session "Leading with Stewardship" on YouTube (or any of his stewardship talks).

3) Look at the 4 F's to determine where you can grow in your stewardship: faith, family, finances, and fitness. How are you stewarding your spiritual growth, your family, your money, and your health? What needs to change?

4) Read *Strengthening the Soul of Your Leadership* by Ruth Haley Barton.

CHAPTER 10:
A LIGHTER LOAD

"My yoke is easy, and my burden is light."
—Matthew 11:30

How is it possible for our work to feel *light*? No pastor we know looks at their work calendar and says, "I've got several light weeks coming up. My job is so easy."

When Jesus speaks to his disciples in Matthew 11, he is literally preparing them for an arduous life's calling. He calls the world to live with a radically different spiritual paradigm than they have ever been presented before—one of stewardship, not ownership. Jesus embodied this concept in his own relationship with his Father:

> » "Don't you believe that I am in the Father, and that the Father is in me? The words I say to you I do not speak on my own authority. Rather, it is the Father, living in me, who is doing his work" (John 14:10).

> "I have testimony weightier than that of John. For the works that the Father has given me to finish—the very works that I am doing—testify that the Father has sent me" (John 5:36).
>
> "I have brought you glory on earth by finishing the work you gave me to do. . . . All I have is yours, and all you have is mine. And glory has come to me through them" (John 17:4, 10).

Jesus knew the work he came to do. He did the work willingly and lovingly. He suffered for his work without complaint or resentment. And he finished his work in the midst of speculation and disbelief.

WHAT SHOULD OUR WORK LOOK LIKE?

John Piper wrote in *Don't Waste Your Life,* "God created us for work so that by consciously relying on his power and consciously shaping the world after his excellence, we might be satisfied in him, and he might be glorified in us."[21] In Genesis 1:27-28, when God creates man and woman—incidentally, to work in cooperation with one another—God immediately gives them work to do: be fruitful and multiply, fill the earth and subdue it, rule over the animals.

In other words, we are destined with a holy calling—a successful work life. Our work should be successful. Just what every workaholic wants to hear!

---

21 John Piper, *Don't Waste Your Life*, Crossway, 2023, 135-136.

But to be obedient and successful workers for God's glory, we must:

- » Reproduce God's spirit (multiply ourselves)
- » Represent God's authority (subdue the earth)
- » Reign in God's supremacy (rule creation)

Work is all about God. It's never about us. Not about who gets the credit, who throws who under the bus, who gets opportunities and who doesn't, who's successful and who's not. None of that matters.

> ## Work is all about God. It's never about us.

The curse on mankind is not work itself (that was a blessing from God). The curse is the toil and struggle to find meaning and authority through our own hard-earned accomplishments. It's the never-ending grind to find significance through accomplishment. In our Western mentality, we assign value to size, control, and influence, yet the Garden of Eden only contains Adam and Eve, who are naked and unashamed. They have no audience, no rivals, and no expectations.

They only have God's directive and companionship. That would have been enough if they had not allowed themselves to be distracted and deceived by the traps of stress and expectation.

They could have stayed yoked to God, engaged in his work, and enjoying his company, unencumbered by the stress of the world.

We always lose our perspective on work when we entertain a deception. "'Did God really say . . . ?'" (Genesis 3:1). *Can you trust God when he seems unfair?*

Probably all of our personal struggles—all of our toxic thinking, emotional spiraling, and fear-based decisions—begin with a similar distortion of God's truth.

Life's not fair.

Someone is taking advantage of me.

We can't trust anyone.

We need to protect ourselves before we get hurt.

If this church doesn't work, I have failed and embarrassed God's name.

Except that none of this life is about us. Jesus' directive in Matthew 11 replicates God's directive from Genesis 1: work with me, not for me.

WHY THE YOKE DOESN'T FEEL EASY

Let's find out why ministry work feels hard instead of easy.

Jesus yokes us to himself, to work with him, to pull straight furrows with him, to complete his mission. We don't have to decide how to pull or where to pull. We just do what he's doing. If we stay connected to him in our work for our entire lives, we will anticipate his every move. We can avoid confusion or dismay whenever he turns or stops. We can work in tandem together.

We should not be surprised, then, by the enemy's tactics to isolate and imprison us with feelings of loneliness, betrayal, and depression. He wants us to pull alone, to one-tenth of our potential. We must decide—and establish ground rules—to work under Jesus' yoke and at Jesus' speed. This may require a change in values.

Let's see how God intends for us to work. In John 14:11-13, Jesus says to his disciples:

> *"Believe me when I say that I am in the Father and the Father is in me; or at least believe on the evidence of the works themselves. Very truly I tell you, whoever believes in me will do the works I have been doing, and they will do even greater things than these, because I am going to the Father. And I will do whatever you ask in my name, so that the Father may be glorified in the Son."*

According to these verses:

» Our work is evidence of the Father's relationship with us
» Our work should clearly point people to the Father
» Our work will be the same as his work, if we believe what we say we believe
» Our work will produce greater results than the miracles that Jesus did

GREATER WORKS

Let's just think about what Jesus possibly meant by *greater works*. The Greek word is *megas*. In Latin, it's translated as *magnum*. This word appears throughout Scripture; one of its closest contexts is in Matthew 8:24, where we find the disciples rowing against a storm on the Sea of Galilee. Matthew records, "Suddenly a furious storm came up on the lake, so that the waves swept over the boat. But Jesus was sleeping." The word for *furious* (or *great* in some translations) is *megas*. It means to be powerful, unmeasurable, abundant, splendid. A final definition reads "of God's preeminent blessing."[22]

This storm is so violent and powerful that the waves are "sweeping across the boat," causing the disciples to be afraid for their lives. Professional fishermen are afraid of this storm (so it's one of the worst they've ever seen). In great distress, they wake Jesus up. He's not alarmed, even though he's soaking and the boat is about to capsize. He has prepared the storm as a growth opportunity for them.

As Sam Chand says, "In *distress*, you find *stress*."[23] When we are buffeted by fears and worries, we are in stress. But we do not have to be *in distress*. Our stress should always point us to preeminent blessing—the Father. If we allow God, he will use every crisis to develop our faith and transform our suffering into blessing, as we respond in dependence and worship.

Without refocusing on God, our stress becomes the tipping point for sin, the point at which we begin to absorb the lies about God, that he is unfair, that he has forgotten us, that he is not enough.

Notice that Jesus *rests* during the storm on the Sea of Galilee before he rebukes it with the famous words: "Peace, be

---

22 Megas, G3172, *Blue Letter Bible*, www.blueletterbible.org/lexicon/g3173/niv/mgnt/0-1

23 Sam Chand, "Rediscovering the Lion in your Leadership," *Stress Test Podcast*, Episode 1, 1 May 2023.

still." Peace is the opposite of chaos, the answer to the disciples' distress.

But the disciples are more terrified by Jesus's power than they were by the storm's fury. "They were amazed and asked, 'What kind of man is this? Even the winds and the waves obey him!'" (Matthew 8:29). They must face their questions: *Is Jesus trustworthy? Is he powerful? Is he God?*

Back to what Jesus said. He tells these same disciples, "You will do *greater works* than these" (John 14:12). You will calm storms. You will quell chaos. You can bring peace amidst terror. When we think about the history of the church, we can notice greater things: the spread of the gospel, the endurance during persecution, the formation of the Church, the translation of the Scriptures, the empowering work of the Holy Spirit.

Later, before Jesus dies, he explains how this miraculous transaction can take place: "And I will ask the Father, and he will give you another Advocate, who will never leave you. He is the Holy Spirit, who leads into all truth. The world cannot receive him, because it isn't looking for him and doesn't recognize him. But you know him, because he lives with you now and later will be in you" (John 14:16).

Then why are we so anxious all the time? Why do we feel burdened by the ministry and unable to live freely in our callings? Read on. In verse 21 of the same chapter, Jesus spells out the hard part: "Those who accept my commandments and obey them are the ones who love me. And because they love me, my Father will love them. And I will love them and reveal myself to each of them" (John 14:21).

What commands did Jesus give us that prove our love?

"Take my yoke upon you. Let me teach you."

Obedience always requires humility, a submission of my will, my expectations, my fear. Obedience, simply stated, is a stewardship issue.

> Obedience, simply stated, is a stewardship issue.

THE MARTYR COMPLEX

We understand the concept: God is God, and we are not.

However, we can easily treat the church like it belongs to us. After all, we perform weddings and funerals. We save marriages and counsel parents through children's crises. We go to the mission fields with one another and worship together. We serve together and pray together. The church is full of our people, and we love them so much it hurts.

But they do not belong to us. We are stewards.

HEALTHY HEARTBEATS FOR "A LIGHTER LOAD":

1) What would make your work lighter? What tasks do you need to offload?

2) Ask your spouse or a key leader to help you identify areas where you could lighten your load and steward your time and talents more effectively.

3) Read *Addicted to Busy: Recovery for the Rushed Soul* by Brady Boyd and *The Emotionally Healthy Church* by Peter Scazzero.

4) Identify one task you guard from anyone's interference. Consider the idolatrous implications of this obsession. Confess it and give to God completely.

PART 3:
A NEW WAY TO REST
(The Redemption of Stress)

"The Lord is my shepherd, I lack nothing. He makes me lie down in green pastures, he leads me beside quiet waters, he refreshes my soul. He guides me along the right paths for his name's sake. Even though I walk through the darkest valley, I will fear no evil, for you are with me; your rod and your staff, they comfort me. You prepare a table before me in the presence of my enemies. You anoint my head with oil; my cup overflows. Surely your goodness and love will follow me all the days of my life, and I will dwell in the house of the Lord forever." —Psalm 23

CHAPTER 11:
THE GOOD SHEPHERD

"The Lord is my shepherd, I lack nothing. He makes me lie down in green pastures, he leads me beside quiet waters. . . ."
—Psalm 23:1-2

Until Shane's heart attack and its subsequent recovery, we had not viewed Psalm 23 as a template for ministry work. It was a template for sadness and grief. A great funeral passage. In fact, Psalm 23 had become so familiar, we had ceased to grasp its deepest meaning.

Verses 1 and 2 of Psalm 23 are perhaps the most-recognized verses in the Bible. David launches a shepherding analogy of comfort and perspective. For us who wander hopelessly, the psalm clarifies the person of God and, therefore, clarifies our own wanting condition.

Jesus is our Savior. Our Friend. Our Bridegroom. Our Beginning and End. Our Way, Truth, and Life. Our Wonderful

Counselor. Even our Prince of Peace, on rare occasions. But let's be honest: we don't always believe that Jesus is our Good Shepherd or that we are his sheep. Our anxiety tells a different story about us.

THE REAL MESSAGE

Let's look at Psalm 23 as a playbook for handling stress. The New Living Translation reads, "The Lord is my shepherd; I have all that I need." In English, "I shall not want" and "I have all that I need" seem to mean two different things. *Not wanting* is usually associated with having abundance—there's nothing else we want out there that we don't already have, so we have no needs. But this verse speaks to the quality of contentment and trust, not to consumerism or abundance of belongings.

Feeling want is a natural human condition. Our sin natures want more, always more. We run ourselves to exhaustion, attempting to secure more because we're honestly fearful that we'll run out of what we need. We're afraid we won't have enough to make us feel secure and happy. We mistakenly think more will make us content.

When we're feeling a lack of time, energy, or affirmation, it's because we've looked for contentment in all the wrong places. *Having all that we need* speaks of contentment and satisfaction irregardless to abundance of things.

Paul addressed our concern about meeting our needs: "Don't worry about anything; instead, pray about everything. Tell God what you need and thank him for all he has done. Then you will experience God's peace, which exceeds anything we can understand. His peace will guard your hearts and minds as you live in Christ Jesus" (Philippians 4:6-7).

There it is again! *His peace will guard your heart.* How?

Do not worry; tell God what you need. Thank him for what he's already provided. Then, you will have peace from the striving, comparing, and pursuing.

We were recently challenged about creating a personal culture where our hearts can thrive. On a long flight to Iceland, we began watching a Netflix documentary, "Live to 100: Secrets of the Blue Zone." Over a period of decades, documentarian Dan Buettner interviewed and compiled data on the areas of the world with the highest concentrations of centenarians, people living past 100 years of age. One of the top five locations is Sardinia, and one of its towns, Acciaroli, boasts a population that includes a shocking 30% of its citizens living beyond 100 years of age.[24]

We were riveted. How did these people live so long?

Buettner's interviews showed that a large number of the Sardinian men over age 90 had been shepherds by trade. Statistically, shepherding ranks as one of the least stressful jobs on the planet. The shepherds he interviewed credited the following reasons for their lack of stress:

- » Physical exercise (walking up and down mountains)
- » Interaction with animals
- » Observation and appreciation of nature's beauty

---

24 Dan Buettner, *Live to 100: Secrets of the Blue Zones*, Netflix, 2023.

- » Slow pace and rest time during the day (when the sheep are resting)
- » Relational interaction with other shepherds
- » Time for reflection and contemplation

According to Sardinian shepherds, daily thoughtful practices create contentment and peace.[25]

In Psalm 23:1, tranquility correlates to openness with God. We lack nothing because we choose to trust God's provision for us. We're not providing for ourselves or through our own intelligence or work ethic. The garden promise for mankind's redemption depended solely on Jesus' eventual arrival—a god-man who, although bit by the serpent, would one day crush its head.

FARM LIFE AND THE CHRISTIAN LIFE

I (Shane) grew up on a horse farm for part of my childhood. We didn't have sheep, and I can tell you why. Sheep need constant supervision. They're oily, noisy, and smelly. They eat everything in their path (we needed the grass for the horses).

Sheep are not bright. Have you ever noticed anyone out walking the cows and horses around, showing them where to eat or drink? Telling the ducks where to swim or the cats where to find mice? No, they can find good food on their own.

But sheep need someone to guide them where to eat, drink, and sleep, or they will hurt themselves. Scripture calls us sheep.

---

25 "Code and Practice for the Care and Handling of Sheep," Appendix E, National Farm Animal Care Council, nfacc.ca/resources/codes-of-practice/sheep/appendix_e.pdf

"We all, like sheep, have gone astray, each of us has turned to our own way" (Isaiah 53:6). We need help.

THE NATURE OF SHEEP

David, so well-acquainted with the world of shepherding, makes some important analogies to help us understand God as our Shepherd.

- » He makes me lie down in green pastures—sheep will unknowingly eat toxic plants, so shepherds guide their sheep toward healthy grazing. In safe pastures, sheep eat freely and without hurry; they also nap safely in fields that the shepherd has chosen for them.
- » He leads me beside quiet waters—shepherds provide fresh and moving streams for their sheep to drink; shepherds will not lead their sheep to deep rivers with dangerous currents.

Throughout Scripture, water represents spiritual refreshment and life. Moses brings water from the rock. The Lord speaks destiny over Hagar then shows her an oasis. Eleazer meets Rachel at a well. Jesus shares the gospel with the Samaritan woman at the same well: "But those who drink the water I give will never be thirsty again. It becomes a fresh, bubbling spring within them, giving them eternal life" (John 4:14, NLT).

> Rest and water are life, and the shepherd finds them for his sheep.

LEARNING TO BE A SHEEP

Jesus regularly uses a shepherding analogy in his teachings, calling himself "the Good Shepherd" and calling his followers "sheep." Even today, church lingo references a pastor as *the shepherd* and his church as *his flock*.

This is where pastors can get tripped up by the analogy. Since we're shepherds, we struggle to be sheep. We must re-look at the comparisons. Notice a few lessons in Scripture to help us see ourselves as sheep who need a shepherd:

- » Knowledge—"the shepherd separates the sheep from the goats" (Matthew 25:32)
- » Intimacy—"I know my sheep, and my sheep know me" (John 10:14)
- » Authority—"The one who enters by the gate is the shepherd" (John 10:2)
- » Unity—"I will strike the shepherd, and the sheep of the flock will be scattered" (Matthew 26:31)
- » Sacrifice—"I am the good shepherd, and the good shepherd lays down his life for the sheep" (John 10:11)

The Good Shepherd | 167

Shepherds understand their sheep in a highly relational manner. A sheep doesn't understand a lot of things, but it knows his shepherd's voice. Sheep feel secure with their shepherd, who doesn't leave them unsupervised (that's the shock value of the parable of the lost sheep). In ancient times, a shepherd slept across the entrance of his sheepfold doorway so no predator or intruder could pass by without encountering the shepherd first.

Sheep want to follow their shepherd. They don't have to be herded like cattle or spurred like horses. They naturally follow the shepherd. Sheep have exceptional hearing. They don't need to be yelled at. In fact, they respond best to soft, reassuring tones.

Sheep also have monocular vision because their eyes are set on the sides of their heads, creating limited frontal vision but good peripheral vision. As they follow the shepherd, they cannot see what's ahead of them, only what's around them. However, when a sheep is grazing with its head down, its vision increases to 360 degrees. A sheep is safest while it's grazing.

Think about it. When a sheep is doing what it's made to do, it functions at premium capacity, with the greatest protection possible.

No sheep turns its head side to side to check its surroundings. It eats the grass it's been brought to eat, and while it eats, it can see everything it needs to see. It's aware of his fellow sheep. When it's time to move on, the sheep follow their shepherd's voice together. While they're moving, they can't see what's happening in front of them, so they depend on the shepherd for their own safety and direction.

Jesus is our Good Shepherd. Because he puts up with us. Because he cares for us. A shepherd is a bit like a parent of young children.

While our children were growing, we naturally had to enforce regular bedtimes because our kids didn't have the maturity to manage their own sleep schedules. Kids run hard until they get overtired and cranky. Exhausted kids whine; they can stumble and hurt themselves; they pick fights with their siblings. They don't eat well or wake up happy.

The best parents are perhaps the parents who gently guide their kids through life without the threats, yelling, insults, or the "silent treatment." Like children, sheep panic if they're pushed or startled. A good shepherd shows compassion and understanding for his sheep's natural inclinations. He knows they can't anticipate danger; they can't stay safe and respond quickly at the same time. So he doesn't pressure them.

That's the enemy's game. Pressure. Push. Frighten.

One of my favorite authors on the Holy Spirit is Elizabeth Alves. In comparing the Spirit's voice to the enemy's deception, she writes, "God leads; Satan drives. God convicts; Satan condemns. God woos; Satan tugs hard."[26] The Good Shepherd doesn't drive his sheep. He leads them.

---

26 Elizabeth Alves, *Becoming a Prayer Warrior*, Regal, 1998, 69.

Without constant supervision, sheep wander off and are lost; they fall down embankments and get injured. They are attacked by predators. Sheep wholly depend on their shepherd for life.

Even though pastors and ministry leaders are spiritual shepherds, God still commands us to behave like sheep. We must understand the paradigm shift that Jesus requires:

- » Be completely familiar with his voice
- » Receive nourishment from what he provides
- » Go where he goes and stay where he stays
- » Do what we've been created to do
- » Trust that he can protect us

Find your field. Find your stream. Follow your shepherd there. Becoming a sheep is a profoundly dependent arrangement. Leaders must prioritize following Christ over leading Christians. You must follow your Shepherd before you can be a shepherd.

> Find your field. Find your stream.
> Follow your shepherd there.

HEALTHY HEARTBEATS FOR "A GOOD SHEPHERD":

1) Quantify contentment. You've heard of counting your blessings. Get specific and enumerate where you find contentment in the Lord. Do it daily. List how your Shepherd provides for you.

2) Spend time with your Shepherd. Bring him your stress and leave with his rest.

3) Read *How Happiness Happens: Finding Lasting Joy in a World of Comparison, Disappointment, and Unmet Expectations* by Max Lucado or *Faith Meets Therapy* by Anthony Evans and Stacy Kaiser, MA, LMFT.

4) Establish regular times for your staff and family to testify of God's blessings, to notice where he's working and celebrate his work.

CHAPTER 12:
REST VERSUS RESTORATION

*"He refreshes my soul. He guides me along
the right paths for his name's sake."*
—Psalm 23:3

Maybe, like us, you've experienced times in ministry where you are flat-out exhausted. You take a well-needed vacation, which you're already worried will not be long enough to send you back refreshed and excited about your work.

Several years ago, we planned a last-minute spring break trip, using timeshare credits and free airline miles for a week in England to watch a soccer game (which ironically got moved to the following week, but that's another story.) Our timeshare exchange was situated in Cornwall, the westernmost county in England, rimmed by a gorgeous rocky coastline of beaches, ruins, and blazing sunsets.

After a half-day flight to Heathrow and a long drive west across the southern countryside, we arrived at night, five times zones away from home, and tumbled into bed. Sue and the boys were up exploring the next morning.

I (Shane) slept for three days.

Literally, I got up each afternoon and went back to bed after dinner. I could not stay awake. My body completely shut down, not like a Sunday afternoon nap, but like I hadn't slept in months. It took leaving the country for my body to fully disengage from stress and engage in restoration. (FYI: That's a massive red flag.)

Rhythms of rest with your Shepherd allow vacations to be for your family, not time to pull you back to normal. Working while being yoked to Jesus is the answer for burnout. It enables us to rest while we work without requiring a drastic change to everything.

> **Working and being yoked to Jesus enables us to rest while we work without a drastic change to our schedule.**

WATER AND THIRST

Let's talk about the language of restoration in Psalm 23:3. In the KJV, the sentence reads, "He restoreth my soul." The NIV translates the verb as "refreshes." It means to "recover; to turn back." This isn't a nap or a gulp of water on a hot day. We know this also because God's not restoring tired limbs or weary eyes or a parched throat. God restores our souls—our hearts—the essence of who we are, what Jesus died to redeem. His restoration is the envigorating baptism of body and spirit, by the power of God, an act of love and rescue that only he understands how much we need.

David uses the word "water" over 50 times in Psalms. When we think of David writing about water, we're reminded of the cave we hiked in Ein Gedi, just west of the Dead Sea. Ein Gedi is the largest oasis in the Judean Desert, a secluded strip of verdancy in the middle of a dry canyon. You can imagine David and his men hunting the deer there and scooping up water to drink.

We hiked the canyon on a trip to Israel. We watched the ibexes (tiny little deer) everywhere, leaping vertically up steep rocks. At the back of the canyon, cold water cascades over the cave's mouth, splashing into a blue pool, streaming down the valley under the shade of olives and pomegranate trees. Here David and his men found fresh water in a secluded hiding place, within sight of the undrinkable Dead Sea, surrounded by an unlivable desert.

In this desolate place, David praised his Lord with words like, "You are my hiding place; you will protect me from trouble and surround me with songs of deliverance." In his desperation, David found God waiting for him in the oasis. The Lord satisfied David's anxious spirit with songs of deliverance and dependence: "As the deer pants for streams of water, so my soul pants for you, my God."

When we're parched, where do we find restoration? Too often, we stay in our palaces and demand justice. We assemble our friends and strategize against our enemies. We do not hike into the quiet canyon and wait for God to speak.

IN THE DESERT PLACE

Where better to thirst for the Lord than when we're in a desert place? What else but insatiable thirst will drive us to seek the Lord?

Remember, David is a shepherd. He knows where to find water and nutrition. Where to sleep, protected against the elements. He trusts his Shepherd. He is willing to lie down in the pastures God leads him to, whatever they look like and however dangerous they may seem.

Saul also knows where the oasis is. He and his soldiers wind their way up the canyon in full view of David's men, who probably hide out in the caves all along the way toward the water source upstream, where David is hidden behind the waterfalls, where he is trapped, with nowhere else to run.

We are never sure where God is leading us, but we know that he never leads us into a trap. Enslavement is the devil's tactic. The Lord grants freedom. We must choose not to reject the freedom he offers just because we can't control the freedom-giver.

God won't force us into restoration. When we avoid places of rest, it's because we have a misunderstanding of who God is and what we need. We convince ourselves that we're not desperate yet; we can hold on a bit longer. We think we just need a day off. A game of golf. A date night. Okay, maybe an exhausting trip across an ocean. That will do it.

It won't.

Rest is preventative. Restoration is curative. Jesus rested; he did not push himself to the point of crashing.

> Rest is preventative. Restoration is curative. Jesus rested; he did not push himself to the point of crashing.

WHEN RESTORATION HAPPENS

If necessary, God will help us rest and be restored. He's okay with us falling into bed for an entire weekend or missing sightseeing with the family because we can't wake up. He can use our spiraling thoughts and crippling depression to whisper his love while we're curled up in the fetal position. He will allow our secret sins to humble us before his holy throne.

God can take any tragedy, calamity, distress, or suffering to redirect your gaze toward his face, to realign your thinking toward his thoughts, and to redirect your love toward his heart's desire. This is the business that God signed up for, willingly. To love flawed humans back into a relationship with himself every time they wander away. He'll do whatever it takes to get our attention. He's proven that already.

Restoration always happens after worship has taken place. David's heart aligns with God's heart because David is a worshiper first. Not a singer. Not a musician.

A worshiper. He unashamedly prostrates himself before God's glory and drinks the living water that satisfies, at personal risk. The restoration process begins here, in God's presence.

What matters to God is a pure heart, not a perfect life. (Again, David proves that.) Psalm 24:3-5 outlines the ideal worshiper, the one who's allowed to enter God's throne room and hear from the Lord. Consider the three requirements for intimacy with God:

» "Clean hands"—none of his works dirty his heart before God
» "Pure heart"—nothing in his integrity interferes with his access to God
» "Does not trust in idols"—nothing competes with God for his heart

The result of intimacy with the Father grants what we all want when we're anxious, afraid, or despairing: "a blessing from the Lord and vindication from God their Savior." We want to be blessed for right, and we want to be exonerated from wrong. Blessing and justice come to the righteous. Righteousness resides in clean hands, pure hearts, and full worship.

WHY REST ALONE DOESN'T WORK

Remember, the word for *restore* is powerful and multi-faceted. It means to "return, recompense, bring back, come back, turn back, refresh, repair, reverse, revoke, pay back." God is a redeemer. He wants to restore us to our designed selves!

God cannot help but restore broken, tired, weary people to the creatures he designed them to be. With God as our Shepherd, we can be confident that his goal and purpose is to restore what we've lost, to redeem what we've destroyed, and to repair what we've broken. Jesus, our Good Shepherd, leads us to safe pastures—not to give us a vacation from the rat race—but to realign all of our disjointed places, to make us whole again.

Rest is repose. Restoration is revitalization. Rest pulls you back from the brink of discouragement until the next time, but restoration prepares you for healthy living and leading.

Rest patches you up. Restoration returns you to wholeness.

Rest is your body working how God designed it to function. Restoration is your soul working how God designed it to work with himself.

How do you get restored?

- » *Consider your intake.* Fill up on God's inspired Word. Read the right books that challenge your soul.
- » *Consider what to offload.* John Maxwell says every year he plans with these three words, "review, reduce, remove."
- » *Worship.* Soak in the presence of Jesus, your Shepherd.

- » *Talk to the right people who fill you.* Find time for a counselor, a coach, a mentor, and encouraging friends (we know there's a difference).
- » *Prioritize solitude.* Find the places that draw you closer to God, where you can spend quality time.

> "He guides me along the right paths for his name's sake." (Psalm 23:3b)

WHICH WAY ARE WE GOING?

David wanders in the wilderness with his fighting men for ten years, waiting for Saul's reign to end. Ten years of visiting the wife (actually *wives*) and kids, then back into hiding. Ten years of brokering deals with neighboring countries to get food and supplies. Ten years of not knowing who to trust. Ten years of raiding enemies and befriending allies. David has committed himself not to kill "the Lord's anointed," so the waiting costs him greatly.

Conversely, Saul has spent those ten years hunting David, suffering from paranoia, anxiety, and depression. He alienates his children; he frightens his loved ones. He repents to David twice but returns to his frantic grasp for control and blessing.

Saul never finds it. He operates outside of God's blessing, without a heart for God's process or plan, and he and his family pay for the stress he cultivates in a heart full of fear. Samuel tells Saul that he could have established a kingdom forever through his godly son Jonathan, but Saul throws it all away because he lives a life of comparison and insecurity. He chooses to live in distress and distrust because he cannot control his circumstances.

Successful, God-honoring leadership demands obedience. Why are we willing to preach the Scriptures, share the gospel, care for the sick, and welcome the outcasts—yet we refuse restoration? We think we can handle the workload, and we think that God is pleased with this.

How misguided and self-destructive.

So God tells us, "Come to me, you who are weary and burdened, and I will give you *restoration*."

FOLLOWING THE VISION

Receiving, communicating, and implementing vision provides one of the most exciting and challenging aspects of leadership. We love hearing from God about where he's taking our organizations, where he's taking us individually. But the process of making it happen can cause enormous stress.

When conflict arises or the numbers plummet, we doubt the path we're on. David says, "He guides me along the right paths for his name's sake" (Psalm 23:3).

We've got to stop and examine a few words here.

» "Right paths"—also translated "paths of righteousness;" this Hebrew word for righteousness translates most often as "justice" or sometimes "vindication." Righteousness is the act of making something that has been wrong right again. Justice. God leads us along paths of justice—he will make the righteous prosper. He will punish the evildoer.

> "For his name's sake"—this is probably the most important part. God will fix our brokenness and make beauty from ashes (a line from Jesus' mission statement in Isaiah 61) to bring glory to himself. Not to us. God's work will honor his own name. We get that messed up a lot. We think our ministry needs to do well so it brings glory to God. It doesn't. When the church is humming along, a lot of celebration happens in our names. We may not be trying to gather praise, but I'm pretty sure we all appreciate the good press. If we truly trusted God with our ministries, we'd lose the competitive and comparative edge that wanting self-glory brings. That's where the stress hides.

HOW TO LEAD LIKE JESUS WHEN YOU'RE FOLLOWING JESUS

"Anyone who wants to be first must be the very last, and the servant of all" (Mark 9:35). The leadership conundrum.

Christian leaders live in an upside-down world. We must continually examine ourselves, our motives, our followers, and our product to determine what kind of shepherd and sheep we are.

> Interpret—know your sheep; know yourself; know your culture; know your call. You must learn to read your surroundings before you can lead your people in a direction.
> Intend—be intentional about your inner circle, your team, and your core; vision must be layered out as the sheep can handle it (most just want to follow the bell and eat).

- » Inspire—find your next leaders and keep them by your side, training and teaching; give them opportunities before they're completely ready because we all learn best from our mistakes; share your load with them.
- » Innovate—learn from everyone above and below you. Learn from other pastors (yep, "the competition"—we're supposed to be on the same team, anyway). Learn from your mistakes; don't be afraid to risk failure—that's how you develop brilliance.

Following Jesus creates leaders who know how to lead, which develops followers who know how to follow. We can avoid organizational pressure and relational distress if we're willing to follow God and rest in his presence. (God doesn't actually need our help. He just loves being close to us.)

Instead of letting our culture and schedules dictate our ministry, we must focus on authentic, personal worship and the direction where it leads us. Then, we will find ourselves in the sanctuary with clean hands, pure hearts, and devoted spirits, hearing from God and doing God's will.

Instead of production, value presence.

Instead of industry, value community.

Instead of praise, value worship.

HEALTHY HEARTBEATS FOR
"REST VERSUS RESTORATION":

1) Read *Restoring Balance to Your Life* by Dr. Richard Swenson and *Leading on Empty: Refilling Your Tank and Renewing Your Passion* by Wayne Cordeiro. Take out your calendar and block off time for restoration: 1 hour/day, 1 day/week, 1 weekend/month, 1 month/year. Plan spiritual retreats, family vacations, and dates (and vacations) with your spouse. Plan rest days on your vacation.

2) Consider blocking off your day into thirds: 8 hours sleep, 8 hours work, 8 hours family and fun.

3) Choose a conduit for restoration (it must be relaxing, not something on your to-do list). Consider:
    » Silence
    » Changes to evening, bed, and waking routines
    » Exercise
    » Art
    » Romancing your spouse
    » Yard work
    » Reading
    » A restful location
    » Music
    » Building, tinkering, or fixing things
    » Diet of healthy food—cut out everything with preservatives
    » A mission trip that you're not leading

CHAPTER 13:

NEW WALK, SAME VALLEY

"Even though I walk through the valley of the shadow of death, I will fear no evil, for you are with me. Your rod and your staff, they comfort me."
—Psalm 23:4

My (Sue's) first memory in life happened around two years of age. I remember sitting on top of my brother (he was four), who was sitting on top of a faceless form lying on the floor. My brother and I were giggling and cheering.

For many years, I didn't realize that it was the only memory I had with my father because he died in a plane crash four months after my second birthday. I remember my grandparents arriving for a visit; instead of scooping us kids up for hugs and kisses, they entered the house crying and embraced my mother. I remember driving away from our house on New Year's Day, leaving behind the tree fort in the backyard. I was looking out the car's back window, surrounded by my stuffed animals and dolls. That was the day we moved away.

I was too young to understand or process our family's grief, but my earliest memories were intertwined with it. I experienced my first valley of the shadow of death, not because I remembered any tragic event but because it became the valley that future griefs would trigger.

My father was a navigator and Lieutenant Colonel in the United States Navy Reserve, as well as a college professor. He died on a training mission in California, but the Navy sealed the crash records, and our family didn't get details. Maybe the Navy didn't know, either. We rarely talked about my dad or his death in our home.

The crash happened in 1969. PTSD was still undiagnosed in soldiers, let alone in families. Nobody saw counselors, if they even existed. Our mother carried our dad's footlocker up to the attic, packed with his uniforms and an assortment of newspaper clippings about his death. She kept his pictures in boxes, not on tables. She put together a new life. We had a happy childhood.

Problem solved.

> "Even though I walk through the valley of the shadow of death, I will fear no evil" (Psalm 23:4a).

Grief stops for no one, and it definitely doesn't vanish because you ignore it. Grief resurfaces in our coping mechanisms, our relationships, our image of God. Grief persists until you fully deal with it. And if you don't give it space to breathe and work itself out, then it doesn't visit anymore—it moves in and dominates your perspectives.

> **Grief persists until you fully deal with it.**

Our country lives in the aftermath of centuries of discrimination, slavery, and war. We still feel the tremors from a global pandemic. Still, our grief surprises us with its debilitating power and its coping mechanisms of avoidance and workaholism.

DEFUSING ABANDONMENT

Your grief and fear return during crisis and attempt to take over your perspective. Whenever I (Sue) feel worried or afraid—whenever I feel attacked, misunderstood, or abused—I emotionally return to being a fatherless child who's worried about how to answer the question, "What does your dad do for a living?" and its follow-up question, "How did he die?" I feel vulnerable, incapable of anticipating people's expectations or satisfying their curiosity about me.

I feel alone.

Grief and trauma always orphan you. That's the go-to call in the devil's playbook. If you settle into an identity of loneliness and emptiness, you remove yourself from feeling connected to a Heavenly Father, who offers all of us adoption and inheritance. You allow the devil to orphan you.

The intimacy and legacy of a father image make sense to people who grew up with dads who played ball and went to father-daughter dances and tucked them in at night with a story. But over half the kids in America didn't grow up like that, and probably half of the pastors didn't, either. Trusting a father doesn't make complete sense to an emotionally orphaned person, even if you understand or relate to a father as a safe and reliable sheltering place. If you feel abandoned by an earthly father, when your world falls apart, your orphaned soul will automatically succumb to the spirit of isolation and self-reliance.

Only the Holy Spirit can heal the wounds from fathering (or the lack of it).

> ### Leaders who lead alone and process alone are orphaned leaders.

Leaders who lead alone and process alone are orphaned leaders. Maybe they struggle with pride or insecurity; most likely, underneath external emotions, lonely leaders have father issues. We all feel disconnected from the Father a lot of the time. Consider these questions to uncover and rebuke the orphan spirit at work in you. Check any that apply to you:

- » Do you long for role models and place high expectations on mentors?
- » Can you point to a list of authority figures who have disappointed you?
- » Are you self-reliant, hard-working, and independent?
- » Do you struggle to ask for advice, take suggestions, or admit you're wrong?
- » Are you naturally suspicious of people's motives or actions?
- » Do you struggle to have close male relationships?
- » Are you often lonely or isolated?
- » Are your decisions influenced by what people think of you?

WALKING IN THE LIGHT AND IN THE SHADOWS

Maybe you're walking through the reality of a loved one's death or a child's devastating mistake. Maybe you're experiencing a crisis in your personal finances or your congregation. You see shadows of darkness in a once-bright life.

Here's the remarkable thing about shadows. They occur because something is blocking the sunlight from reaching the earth, like a building, mountain, or cloud. Instead of hitting the ground, the sun is blocked by an object, which then casts a shadow over the ground. These shadows are directly proportional to the angle at which sunlight touches the earth. The lower the sun's arc (i.e., the farther the sun is from Earth), the longer the shadow grows.

Just like us. The farther we get from God's presence, the longer our shadows grow.

Now for the cool part. Direct sunlight dispels shadows. If you are experiencing a valley of shadows, that means the sun is close by; it's just hidden by something large.

But the sun is still present. It's shining. It's moving. That blocking object won't always cover you in darkness. You must keep walking until you emerge from the shadow of the big, terrible thing.

Our soul shadows become obvious whenever the Son shines. His Spirit shows us reality. "God is light; in him there is no darkness at all. If we claim to have fellowship with him and yet walk in the darkness, we lie and do not live out the truth. But if we walk in the light, as he is in the light, we have fellowship with one another, and the blood of Jesus, his Son, purifies us from all sin" (1 John 1:5-7).

A good shepherd leads his sheep into the light. While the sheep may pass through dark places, the shepherd won't leave them in the shadows, exposed and afraid. Remember that in Psalm 23, restoration happens *before* the crisis. The sheep (and the shepherd) rest *before* they walk through the valley of the shadows. They're alert and prepared for the valley. The shepherd carries his weapons with him: a rod, a staff, and, in David's case, a slingshot. The shepherd is watchful as he leads his sheep through the shadows; that's why the sheep aren't afraid.

FIGHT FEAR

The New International Version records fear in the Bible in 717 references. (The word for *fear* is used 336 times, *afraid* is used 205 times, *worry* is used 15 times, and *concern* is used 161 times.) God understands that we have fear, that we need to process fear, and that we can overcome fear. Fear is not a leadership weakness; it's an opportunity for faith. Scripture contains many examples of leaders who mishandled their fear. Fear seizes us when we feel:

- » Guilty (Genesis 3:10)
- » Trapped (Genesis 18:15)
- » Weak (Genesis 31:31)
- » Overwhelmed (Joshua 8:1)
- » Unsafe (1 Samuel 22:23)
- » Unworthy (2 Samuel 6:9)
- » Insecure (2 Samuel 14:15)

Fear occurs whenever we focus on our own capabilities. As spiritual leaders and children who are adopted by God, we must address our residual fear of not belonging before we can effectively do the work of the ministry. Healthy leaders build healthy churches. Unhealthy leaders build unhealthy churches. Brené Brown says in *Dare to Lead*, "Leaders must invest a reasonable amount of time attending to fears and feelings, or squander an unreasonable amount of time trying to manage ineffective and unproductive behavior."[27]

---

[27] Brené Brown, *Dare to Lead*, Random House, 9 October 2018.

Every time God calls you to a new initiative, the devil will launch an attack to stop you; when you obey and experience God's power, the devil will launch an attack to diminish it. All his attacks are based on your understanding of who God is. He will try to make you doubt that God is good, that God is caring, and that God is capable. He will tell you that God is not a Father to be trusted. He will use your own experiences against you.

Our bodies were designed to exist in peace and harmony with God (remember your original purpose), so when we experience fear or panic, that's the body telling us to stop and notice that something is misaligned. The devil authors chaos; God authors peace. Don't be tempted to put a band-aid on your chaos and fear. Don't push through it. Trace your fear back to its source and eliminate it with faith—God has designed you for peace and unity with him.

FIGHT ISOLATION

Isolating you is the devil's strongest move for removing you from God's blessing and calling. Whenever you operate alone, you lose the kingdom perspective. Always, the devil plots to pit people against you—even good people—to push back your vision, to sterilize your passion. The enemy of God hyper-focuses on deceiving spiritual leaders to lead alone, especially through their valleys.

God only operates in community. He is a trinity, in constant community with himself. God basks in intimacy with us. He sent his Son to die for the whole world so that we would never be isolated from him, on this earth or for eternity. He designed

New Walk, Same Valley | 191

the church to be a functioning body of unique members so that nobody lives and grows alone.

We have a slogan at our church that we say every Sunday in service: "Nobody walks alone." Our members shoulder-tap people raising their hands for salvation and walk the aisle with them. We assign Connectors to befriend anyone new to faith, to hang out with them, sit with them, bring them to events and fellowships. Without community in the body, how do we expect anyone to feel God's love?

Isolation and loneliness are absolutely counter-productive to God's design for a pastor's life and mission. If you feel completely alone—and 65% of pastors do—your body will send you signals that it can't hold on any longer, that it's going to crash.

Pay attention to the signals.

Lonely leaders are generally not leaders devoid of friends or resources—they are leaders trapped in self-protection. They have walled themselves off from vulnerability and threat in an effort to avoid pain or silence trauma. They are doing their personal best to keep the machine going, to work hard for the kingdom, to keep from leaving the ministry. But they—and we mean *you and us*—are going to crash.

Loneliness won't protect you. Believe us, we've tried it quite a few times. We've readjusted the friendship layers. We've been in and out of small groups. We've had go-to Friday-night couples and no Friday-night couples. We've gone to every event, and we've popped into events and sneaked home. We've sat alone in our living room and wondered, "Can we trust anyone anymore?"

Warning! You are living in the shadows of death. Your anxiety is going to kill something: you, your ministry, your faith, your marriage, your kids' faith. Something—maybe everything—is engaged in dying.

WHAT'S YOUR VALLEY?

Psalm 23:4 is a comforting verse at funerals because grieving people can't imagine a life beyond what they've known before. Loss frightens us. It might be the hardest part of pastoring. People leave us, and we have no control over it.

As pastors, we manage loss for ourselves and others much more than we should. We have conversations with our people whenever we make changes to church programs, styles, personnel, environment, or vision. We help our people process their personal losses—divorce, death, estrangement, retirement, joblessness, bankruptcy, and disappointment. We face our own losses with staff transitions, attendance migration, and financial insecurity.

> All pastors experience leadership pain.

All pastors experience leadership pain. We experience highs and lows. We all understand betrayal, fear, insecurity, and anxiety in the ministry. If we all sat together in a circle and shared our worst church experiences, we would all nod at one another, a brotherhood and sisterhood of hurt and toil and tiredness. Our eyes would fill with tears. We would say, *Yes, that's happened to me.*

This is why community and vulnerability among pastors are so important. We must walk with each other through the uncertain spaces. Pain can either function as the enemy's process to alienate us from God or God's process to realign our hearts to him. When we are willing to share our pain with one another, he leads us safely through the valley. Decide if you're operating in alienation or alignment. Then you'll know who you're following through the valley.

> "Your rod and staff, they comfort me" (Psalm 23:4b).

The shepherd in Psalm 23 carries something while he's shepherding. Maybe he's got a slingshot, but David doesn't mention it in Psalm 23. The shepherd here—who's a metaphor for God—carries shepherding tools: a rod and a staff. That's the kind of Father-God we have. He doesn't walk around with a slingshot. He doesn't need it. But he uses the rod and staff.

THE ROD AND STAFF

Symbolically, the rod and staff represent authority, compassion, and comfort. The rod represents authority, like a king's scepter. The staff has a crook on one end for rescuing sheep who had fallen into crevasses. With the crook, a shepherd can also stretch out his staff and guide lambs back to their mothers or pull sheep back onto the path or into the herd. A shepherd lays the staff flat across a sheep's back while they walk together, which reinforces a physical connection of the shepherd to the sheep.

God's rod and staff identify us as the object of his affection. The rod brings correction, and the staff brings us direction. Both are tools of comfort, but correction and direction are signs of intentional care. Every loving parent utilizes correction and direction as they shepherd their children. This is discipleship.

We are never alone in our valleys.

FIGHT ANXIETY

Nobody ever cross-stitched "Be resilient" on a pillow.

"Be anxious for nothing"—*yes*.

"Don't sweat the small stuff"—*yes*.

But never "Be resilient." Resilience implies endurance, fatigue, suffering, and longevity; nobody's particularly inspired and comforted by those concepts.

But resilience is the antidote for anxiety. Telling ourselves to have more faith isn't wrong, but it doesn't help us run the race. We must acquire enough faith to reduce stress and fulfill what God called us to.

We must develop resilience.

Resilience isn't just grit or pluck or fortitude. Resilience is the acceptance of suffering and the adaptation to it. Resilience is a reality check about loss and gratitude. Something in life has changed—something has been lost—and we can get stuck in our sorrow, or we can move forward. But we can't go back.

Moving on might be the hardest part of ministry. Calling doesn't mean a job. You might not stay at the same place or shepherd the same people. God calls people to other places, and he calls us to other places because he is writing a bigger story than we can see. Your stress might be a sign that God is calling you from something to something. Maybe another ministry. Maybe another city. Maybe another way of living. Certainly, he is calling you to a lighter yoke and stiller waters. God always calls us out of chaos into peace.

Resilience develops slowly and intentionally by leaning into God's character, which never changes. This is why we must do the work to figure out what we really believe about God and our current situation. Do we expect God to go easy on us because we're good people? Because we shepherd the flock?

WHAT'S YOUR CORE BELIEF ABOUT GOD? BE HONEST.

Your core belief about God's character will carry you through any crisis. That's it. It's that simple and that complicated. What do you honestly believe about God when cancer strikes or when an accident cripples your status quo?

We know and believe God works all things together for good. He turns ashes to beauty. He infuses life into dry bones. He raises the dead. But he never, ever changes something to its original state. Not even us. Even eternity will be different than creation: we will live with God in our celestial bodies, redeemed and sanctified by Christ's sacrifice. That's not the same as Adam and Eve before the fall.

In a crisis—especially in a crisis that lasts for months or years—your theology will support or demolish your faith. This is why we pastors leave the faith, why we blow up our families, why we deconstruct the Church. We can easily believe something about God that isn't completely true. And when life doesn't turn out like we expect it to, we end up demolishing the whole system.

Here's the safeguard for your faith: "And the peace of God, which transcends all understanding, will guard your hearts and your minds in Christ Jesus" (Philippians 4:7). We cannot and must not veer from the core belief that God is good and he does good. He is love.

Love does good, no matter the cost.

Isaiah 43:19 is one of our favorite passages, especially during the shadowed valleys of our life: "See, I am doing a new thing! Now it springs up; do you not perceive it? I am making a way in the wilderness and streams in the wasteland."

This is how God works. He is always working in places we can't see. He engages in the action of redemption and restoration, and he invites us to notice the signs and believe in the future.

IN ANOTHER CANYON

Forty-four years after my father died, I (Sue) found an aviation archeologist on the internet who had personally excavated the site of my father's plane crash. Shane and I booked a flight. We met the archeology crew. We paged through a binder of research. Someone knew what happened. Someone cared.

We stood overlooking three valleys in southern California, all strewn with plane wreckage. We saw the airbase, only four miles away through the hazy sky. We lingered at the point of impact. I sat in a seat, dinged but completely intact, on the canyon floor. A plane wing stretched across the mountainside beyond. Pieces of the fuselage littered the hillsides. A million pieces of shrapnel told the story of explosion and devastation.

We memorialized my father's life. We respected the sacrifice. We experienced the intimacy of that place and the suffering that had occurred there.

Most importantly, I felt my father there. Down in the valley of the shadow of death, my Father-God walked with me and led me back into the light.

HEALTHY HEARTBEATS FOR "NEW WALK, NEW VALLEY":

1) Take the "Fight Fear Assessment" in the Resources in the back of the book. This chart can help you identify your fears and replace the embedded lies with the truth of Scripture.

2) Read *Father Hunger* by Robert S. McGee.

3) Share the gospel with someone; spend time with new believers. Nothing corrects your perspective on life better than seekers and new believers.

4) Get a professional grief counselor or grief therapist; go regularly.

5) Invite pastors (and their spouses) to get coffee or lunch with you. Find out how they're doing. Share, empathize, encourage. Become friends.

CHAPTER 14:
A SEAT AT THE TABLE

"You prepare a table before me in the presence of my enemies. You anoint my head with oil; my cup overflows."
—Psalm 23:5

HOW WE COME TO THE TABLE

None of us want stories of brokenness. We want to see God's glory magnified in our lives, but we want it to happen without pain. Without an audience. We all hope to walk through life unscathed, victorious, and joyful.

Spoiler: it doesn't work out that way for anyone. Some of us are just better actors.

We all try to keep our failures hidden. We rewrite our leadership blunders. We embellish outcomes. When we're invited into the open—when we're required to show up and engage—we come with our best manners, our smiles and gratefulness, our tried-and-true stories, our best small talk and listening skills. We come to make a good impression and get out of there before something bad happens to us.

We hide our little addictions because we tell ourselves they're not so damaging. We're coping with our stress as best as we can. We tell ourselves we're not hurting anyone. The important thing for our church and our family is that we keep everything together so we don't explode.

We hide our brokenness out of shame and pride. We believe the lie that brokenness discredits the kingdom of God, even though our brokenness magnifies God's glory. We regret our histories, stuffing them deep down because we don't want to be another person with a tale of woe. Another son or daughter with father issues. Another child of divorce. Another abused child. Another spouse who's been cheated on. Another leader who's fallen into sin.

Our fear has taught us not to be those people, even if we are. We know that Paul boasted in his weaknesses. He admitted to being a murderer of Christians, yet he expected them to obey him as their apostle. But rather than hide his past, he allowed God to receive all the glory for his transformed life. He decided, perhaps during those three years in the wilderness with Jesus, to lay down all notions of managing his narrative or preserving his reputation. He embraced humiliation so that he could say, "I have been crucified with Christ and I no longer live, but Christ lives in me. The life I now live in the body, I live by faith in the Son of God, who loved me and gave himself for me" (Galatians 2:20).

EVERYTHING IMPORTANT HAPPENS AT THE TABLE

The family table holds a special place in our home. It might be the biggest holder of memories. It's where we eat, play board games, hold family discussions, entertain friends and acquaintances, pray together, tell funny stories, laugh with (and at) each other, and celebrate special days.

Our boys used the kitchen table to build Legos, read books, do artwork, apply to colleges, read mail, plan life-changing moments. Our table has witnessed us doing our best and most loving work.

But we also argue at the table. Countless times, we have confronted misbehavior, taught table manners, and corrected the boys about being bad winners and losers. We have struggled with them, supervising homework assignments and reviewing for tests. We've gotten out of our seats to hug them, to wipe their tears, to pray over them. At the table, we've paid bills and panicked over problems and argued about whose fault something was. We've processed mistakes, pain, and grief at the table. We've apologized and forgiven one another there.

The family table is a haven after a hard day. If you're healthy and your family is healthy, the table is such a safe place. You come together and you listen to one another. You share your highs and lows. Your dreams and sorrows. You cheer for one another.

So how loaded is the imagery when David says to God, "You prepare a table before me . . ." The Hebrew word for *table* doesn't refer to your average meal in an ancient dwelling. The word suggests the king's table, a splendid feast spread out, hundreds of place settings lined up across from one another. The table is a banquet, an honored gathering where everyone celebrates abundance.

As the special event table-preparer in our family, preparing a banquet requires many days of thoughtful planning and working. Today, I (Sue) have been planning Thanksgiving dinner for our immediate and extended family in the area. Although everyone brings something, I'm the hostess, so I'm most responsible for most of the meal. I prepare all the basics: turkey, ham, stuffing, gravy, drinks, a couple of sides, and dessert. I'll clean my house (especially the bathrooms) and set up a second table in order to double our current seating capacity. We bring down more chairs from the attic. I lay out linens, china, glassware, cloth napkins, flowers, and candles. We blow the leaves off the yard.

After an all-too-quick dinner of delicious food and delightful conversation, I'll spend more hours cleaning up, washing pots and pans, throwing the linens in the washing machine, putting away all those platters and baking dishes I rarely use. The china and silver will go back into their designated locations in the hutch.

Something magical happens when we're all bringing food to the banquet table, when everyone samples each other's dishes and gets up for second helpings. Love and belonging spark inside me when my grown sons circle back for the pie and cookies they remember from their childhood. Each of us tell stories about the recipes and the person who used to make it. We remember previous holidays and the people we shared them with.

Thanksgiving isn't truly about the food. It's about food memories that activate our prefrontal cortexes and remind us of the people we love and miss. The dinner table means family. It shows everyone that they belong, that they're important enough for someone to do the work to satisfy their cravings. They're important enough to set aside the time to play and eat and talk and love.

> The dinner table means family. It shows everyone that they belong, that they're important enough for someone to do the work to satisfy their cravings.

This is what our Lord does for us. He prepares a feast. He sets a table. And he seats us next to himself. We're at the King's table because no matter what people say about us—no matter how awful other dinner tables may have made us feel before—here we are safe. God says we are worthy of his love and his sacrifice.

THE SURPRISE ATTACK

Now for the confusing phrase "in the presence of my enemies."

Have you ever felt like you were surrounded by your enemies at a table you thought was safe?

We've probably all been surprised by a meeting with an old friend or colleague, maybe even a respected mentor. One fine day, in a restaurant or even in your own home, someone said something about how they were disappointed in you as a leader or how "It's not personal, but..."

And your heart broke.

You heard it crack.

You felt nauseous. The heat rose into your cheeks, and your hands went cold.

Instead of asking questions or offering to pray for you, someone you trusted crossed the divide into the space reserved for people who hurt you.

You felt completely isolated, judged, and misunderstood.

And the devil whispered that you've ruined everything or that you were never good enough. He tells you to hide. Or retaliate. Do anything to escape this feeling of failure and loss because nothing good can come of this horrible situation. Your table—your meeting place—was no longer safe.

EATING WITH THE ENEMY

What kind of king would invite your enemies to a celebration dinner?

We don't like to think about anyone being our "enemy." We're in the redemption business. We might censure politicians or local businesses whose actions defame the message of the gospel, but we work to create friends within the Church.

Enemy is a strong word. Way too dramatic for a spiritual person to use.

Yet David uses it freely throughout the Psalms. Sure, he's literally running for his life—not something we have to think about in Western Christianity. But David's laments and requests to God embody more than a temporary solution to his present suffering. David turns to God to restore his identity, his reputation, and his calling.

Although David suffers from a list of intimate betrayals during his lifetime, King Saul tops the list. David gives Saul love, respect, honor, and comfort, and Saul tries to kill him. Again and again.

On the surface, they start off well enough. Saul invites David to eat at his dinner table and live in the palace. Saul gives David position and wealth. He gives David his daughter to marry. He depends on David to calm his mental health.

But Saul makes David his enemy because he is

» Afraid for his reputation
» Convicted of his sin
» Confused about his calling
» Ambitious for his legacy

Saul's actions resemble the "enemy attacks" we encounter on a regular basis inside our churches and ministries. Saul violates his promises to David; he exploits their relationship; he envies David's success; he leverages his power against David; he traumatizes David and his family. He completely mismanages and mangles his position as the steward of God's people, all because he feels threatened by a young man who experiences God's favor and blessing on his life.

Remember that attacks come from fear, from schoolyard bullies who have deep wounds and are afraid they won't belong, aren't appreciated, and can't control their future. People—even good people—lash out against you because they've buried their gold in the ground and they want you to bury yours because it makes them feel less guilty.

Most of our "enemies" are people who disagree with our ideas or perspectives because they've got their own overwhelming stress. Their words and actions don't physically endanger us, but the stress we absorb from them will.

NOT YOUR FAULT

Could you have made different decisions and avoided attacks against you?

Maybe. Probably. We would make a lot of different decisions in life once we find out what happens in the end. Our mistakes don't matter. God is a God of the future—he is always making things new. He is always redeeming our mistakes and our pain.

The reality about enemies is this: good leaders repent and humble themselves when they uncover an offense. Enemies don't. Enemies allow the devil to get a foothold in their hearts and minds. They fill the holes in their soul by transferring blame onto someone else, someone more visible than them (a.k.a. their leader). They sit at the table and hear half the conversation. They miss the heart behind your decisions and the calling behind your strategies. They use the greatest weapon available: intimacy.

The Hebrew word for *enemy* in Psalm 23:5 is interesting. It's not a noun. It's a verb, *sarar*. It means "to distress, vex, afflict, bind up, to show hostility."[28] The previous phrase "in the presence" is *neged,* meaning "to be conspicuous, in front of, opposite of."[29] The idea is *in your face.*

Think about verse five a little.

We're sitting at a nice dinner *with the source of our stress in our faces.*

> We're sitting at a nice dinner with the source of our stress in our faces.

It doesn't seem like a good plan. God plans a banquet for us. He seats us close to him. Then he allows those who have hurt us to be there, too.

All the while, our Father-God engages us in loving conversation with us at the table *where we feel safe*. When we're seated with him, we have family conversation. We share. We tease. We feast. You see, intimacy is not threatened by the enemy's

---

28 Sarar, H6887, Psalm 23:5, *Blue Letter Bible*, https://www.blueletterbible.org/lexicon/h6887/niv/wlc/0-1/

29 Neged, H5048, Psalm 23:5, *Blue Letter Bible*, https://www.blueletterbible.org/lexicon/h2617/niv/wlc/0-1/

presence. If anything, like a good parent, God's presence near our enemies makes them shrink in their seats. Moses uses the word *sarar*, meaning *enemy,* as an action in Exodus 23:22. God is giving Israel all his specific commandments: "If you listen carefully to what he says and do all that I say, I will be an enemy to your enemies and will oppose those who *oppose* you." In other words, God will *distress* anyone who tries to *bind you in distress*. God's not talking about those who disagree with you, but rather those who take positions against you personally. Those who stand against you and work to hurt you. Your enemy is his enemy.

In 2 Kings 5:23, *sarar* appears in the context of urging or compelling someone. Naaman *binds* Gehazi to take his gifts to Elisha, following Naaman's healing in the Jordan River. Naaman puts stress on Gehazi to take the gifts, but at this point in the story, Gehazi has lied to Naaman by saying that Elisha changed his mind and wants the clothing and silver to give to two other prophets. (Of course, Gehazi intends on keeping them for himself.) Think about the implications of vexing someone to do something. Pressure creates a stressful, binding situation, a situation caused by the sin of an enemy.

So. God will vex, afflict, bind up, and show hostility to those who vex, afflict, bind up, and show hostility to us. Every time David begs God to slay his enemies, David isn't being revengeful. He's reminding God of what God has already promised to do.

> "You anoint my head with oil; my cup overflows" (Psalm 23:5-6).

"Anoint my head with oil" is an interesting Hebrew phrase. It literally means, "you have made fat the leader." God makes a public display of choosing and elevating us, not for our own glory but for his.

Instead of holding a private ceremony or having an intimate family dinner, God publicly anoints you as his chosen leader. Yes, our churches imitate this practice when we commission missionaries and vote in pastors. Those ceremonies and services encourage our church family and embolden leaders to step forward in faithful ministry. We hold these ceremonies in the environment of celebration and thanksgiving; our hearts fill with love and expectation. In Psalm 23:5, David paints the picture of King (God) filling the room with hostile observers at a feast where the guest of the king (us) is honored and sanctified in his position and calling.

The overflowing cup represents abundance, extravagance, and bounty. Notice how John the Apostle sat at an intimate table next to Jesus in the presence of an enemy. John leaned in and asked Jesus questions. He tried to understand Jesus' confusing words about Peter's betrayal. He thought Judas was their friend.

John endured Jesus' trial and crucifixion up close. In the valley of the shadow of death, he faced his greatest fears and took responsibility for Jesus' mother. John ran into the empty tomb and believed in the resurrection. Later, he writes explaining God's extravagant love to believers like this: "See what great love the Father has lavished on us, that we should be called children of God! And that is what we are! The reason the world does not know us is that it did not know him" (1 John 3:1).

Don't come to the table afraid. God gives to overflowing. He gives love "to the full" (John 10:10). In Ephesians, Paul writes about the purpose of God's abundant love: knowing him. Intimacy at his table.

> *"I pray that out of his glorious riches he may strengthen you with power through his Spirit in your inner being, so that Christ may dwell in your hearts through faith. And I pray that you, being rooted and established in love, may have power, together with all the Lord's holy people, to grasp how wide and long and high and deep is the love of Christ, and to know this love that surpasses knowledge—that you may be filled to the measure of all the fullness of God" (Ephesians 3:16-19).*

Nothing diminishes an enemy's influence so fast as when you realize he's already been defeated. That you are fully and sacrificially loved by an all-powerful king. That he has no authority over you or the abundance in your future. That your valley is a pass-through to eternal blessing, a mere shadow cast by the loving works of the Son.

ACTION STEPS FOR "A SEAT AT THE TABLE":

1) Read *Don't Give Your Enemy a Seat at the Table* by Louie Giglio.

2) Prioritize table time with family and friends. Practice affirming and listening. Talk about "highs" and "lows" from the day. Lay hands and pray over one another.

3) Analyze your "table time" at work. Make sure your staff feels safe at the table, desk, or conference room with you. Ask them how you can improve meetings to make everyone comfortable with vulnerability, suggestions, and critique. Covenant together to be honest and kind in your disagreements.

4) When you disagree with your spouse or a collegue, fight fair. Lay the ground rules. Create a safe environment. Listen carefully. Make sure you understand. Affirm your love for them.

CHAPTER 15:

THE HOUSE OF THE LORD

"Surely, goodness and mercy will follow me all the days of my life, and I will dwell in the house of the Lord forever."
—Psalm 23:6

In a meeting with Scott Wilson several years ago, I (Shane) said—with all the passion of a new lead pastor who had big dreams—"I would do anything for my church. No matter what it took. I love this church. I would die for it!"

Scott almost leaped at me. "No!" he exclaimed. "That's not your job. Don't ever say that! Jesus already died for the church; he doesn't want you to die for it."

He's right. Why am I letting my calling kill me?

Staying in your current ministry is a separate question from staying in your calling.

Your church didn't call you into the ministry. They just hired you.

God called you to ministry.
Don't quit your calling.

> Don't quit your calling.

You may need to do some soul-searching and serious listening to hear what God is telling you to do in your valleys and on your mountaintops. Counselor and psychotherapist Jeremy J. Lanning says, "When you quit the known, you also quit the unknown."[30] You'll never know what is on the other side of your valley unless you walk through the shadows. God is leading you toward his preferred future for you. If you stop following him, you won't experience the abundant blessing he wants to unleash after you've learned from him during this season of your leadership.

SURELY GOODNESS AND MERCY

Goodness and *mercy* are the two powerful Hebrew words, *tobe* and *hesed*. *Goodness* has the idea of wealth, beauty, and prosperity; mercy, or lovingkindness. *Hesed* carries the idea of kindness and faithfulness. *Hesed* is used throughout the Old Testament, often coupled with immediate, actionable results.[4]

» Rahab shows *hesed* to the spies; they save her family during the assault on Jericho (Joshua 2:11-12).

---

[30] Jeremy J. Lanning, LPC, CCTP, Conversation, 19 August 2021.

- » Boaz shows *hesed* to Ruth; then he buys her debt and marries her (Ruth 2:20).
- » Jonathan loves David, so David shows *hesed* to Jonathan's son, Mephibosheth (2 Samuel 9:7).

As in these stories and so many others, lovingkindness and mercy follow the person who shows lovingkindness and mercy. The merciful receive mercy (Matthew 5:7) in the midst of injustice and persecution. Mercy is not required any other time; it's required when someone behaves like an enemy. The Sermon on the Mount radically portrays the kingdom of heaven, a spiritual paradigm requiring intimacy with God. The kingdom of heaven operates outside of human logic or self-will.

We need to experience goodness and mercy in order to offer goodness and mercy. By accepting the abundant love of God, I can experience and extend goodness and mercy in this life ("all the days of my life"), as well as the next life ("I will dwell in the house of the Lord forever").

IN MY FATHER'S HOUSE

John records Jesus' last words of comfort to the disciples before Jesus faces his trial and crucifixion. He describes a home, and he promises to take them there to live with him. Jesus is the Bridegroom, after all. He must go and prepare a home for his Bride, the Church. Then without warning, Jesus will return for his Bride and take her away forever. He will bring her to safety, to a new and indescribable future of relationship and intimacy.

Jesus begs his disciples to discard their stress and fear. He knows they can't understand what's happening, so he asks them to trust him. "Do not let your hearts be troubled. You believe in God; believe also in me. My Father's house has many rooms; if that were not so, would I have told you that I am going there to prepare a place for you? And if I go and prepare a place for you, I will come back and take you to be with me, that you also may be where I am."

Trust Jesus. He's preparing something better for you. Something lavish and eternal. Everything here is temporary and preparatory. Be sure you're following God, not the voices of people who love you or the people who don't. They are responsible to hear God's voice for them, not God's voice for you.

Your body, soul, and spirit are speaking to you. Your spouse, kids, mentors, and leaders are speaking to you. The Holy Spirit is speaking to you. Are you in a solid place of restoration so you can distinguish the voice of God when it speaks through people? Can you distinguish others' opinions when they do not reflect God's voice?

God's pathway is difficult. He's never been covert about his calling or his mission. It's difficult. The kingdom of heaven is also difficult; it's a pearl of great expense. It's a treasure hidden in the ground. It's an upside-down way of living. Here are some practical suggestions for staying in the will of God as a healthy leader:

- » God always leads us in upward mobility; stewardship begets greater stewardship.

- » God leads us through dark valleys to restoration on the other side (pain is always for God's glory).
- » God opens doors and shuts doors; don't allow other people to define your pathways.
- » The devil moves and speaks with chaos, harm, confusion, and fear; God doesn't. You can't "trust your gut" if it's not healthy.
- » Stepping out in faith means not having a Plan B; that's why it's faith.
- » Listening to God means blocking out all the other voices; God doesn't work in committee.

Whatever God's call looks like for you, this much is true: he did not call you to die for anything temporal. He promised eternal reward.

When we live and lead in stress, when we nurture stress and excuse stress and—heaven help us, feel proud of our stress, we are essentially climbing Calvary's hill and saying, "Jesus wasn't enough. I'll help Jesus save and grow my church." Instead of taking up our crosses and following him, we pull out his cross and complain about how heavy it is. How overwhelming it is. How we just can't do this anymore.

We were never supposed to carry his cross. We're supposed to carry our own crosses.

Dying for the Church is Jesus' calling and the destiny he already fulfilled. Let death come by sharing the gospel for your whole entire life. Let us claim "For to me, to live is Christ and to die is gain" And mean it about our purpose, not about our ministry. Do not suffer death by pastoring or death by self-neglect. Only one Shepherd should give his life for his sheep.

The rest of us should give our lives for him.

HEALTHY HEARTBEATS FOR "THE HOUSE OF THE LORD":

1) Identify your growth team—counselor, coaches, mentors, prayer warriors, and friends.

2) Take the stress test and regularly examine your physical, emotional, mental, and, of course, spiritual well-being. But please don't stop with the spiritual. You are not a healthy leader if you only care for your soul.

3) Identify self-care, soul-care, and growth habits and rhythms. Keep working at it until you get a good rhythm.

4) Plan your sabbath.

5) Find resources. Subscribe to *Stress Test* Podcast by texting "stress" to 833-204-2158.

6) Interact with us via email, Facebook, or Instagram.

OTHER RESOURCES BY SHANE AND SUE SCHLESMAN

Stress Test: The Heartbeat of a Healthy Leader Podcast
with Shane and Sue Schlesman

Soulspeak: Praying Change into Unexpected Places (Selah Winner 2020)
by Sue Schlesman

Best of Friends
by Susan Walley

Coming in 2024:
The Compassion Bible Storybook by Crystal Bowman and Sue Schlesman

RESOURCES

STRESS ASSESSMENT

Mental Impact: Do you experience any of the following?
- ❑ Poor cognitive functions
- ❑ Trouble concentrating
- ❑ Trouble remembering
- ❑ Pessimism
- ❑ Difficulty making decisions

Physical Impact: Do you experience any of the following?
- ❑ Fatigue
- ❑ Skin or nerve conditions
- ❑ Lowered immunity
- ❑ Poor sleep
- ❑ Headaches
- ❑ Upset stomach
- ❑ Muscle tension

Emotional Impact: Do you experience any of the following?
- ❏ Mood swings
- ❏ Increased anxiety
- ❏ Increased irritability
- ❏ Easily angered
- ❏ Depression
- ❏ Increased impatience
- ❏ Increased nervousness

Spiritual Impact: How do you feel about God?
- ❏ Distant
- ❏ Angry
- ❏ Forgotten
- ❏ Indifferent
- ❏ Confused

# FINDING THE SOURCE OF YOUR STRESS

What triggers your stress anxiety and stress in your personal and professional lives?

Directions: On the next page, circle any statement that applies to you on a regular basis. Look up the Scriptures, pray over them, and commit them to memory.

Trigger	Trigger	Trigger
You have friends who said they'd never leave your church but left anyway	You've ministered sacrificially to people who then go somewhere else to "be fed"	You hesitate to be vulnerable & fully yourself around people
You were wronged by someone who won't admit it, and the injustice eats at you	You assume that people will hurt you; you don't trust anyone completely	You feel hurt whenever you think about someone who hurt you
Your ministry is not growing to the standards you have set	You're embarrassed by your mistakes	You are crushed when people criticize you or compare you to another pastor
You often think about quitting or changing careers	You want to avoid talking to church people	You have insomnia, exhaustion, or feel depressed
You worry a lot, about money, your family, your health, your ministry success	You dread confrontation, correction, board meetings, emails from congregants	Your heart rate and blood pressure are often rapid; you rely on self-medication to calm down
You're critical & judgmental of others	You work hard to be "perfect" and "excellent" in everything	You carry secrets about things you don't want anyone to know about you
You don't have close friends	You only feel safe at home	You protect yourself and your family from intimate relationships in the church
You are often angry at yourself about who you are and how you lead	You obsess about your mistakes	You wish you could make different decisions than you've made

Possible Root Cause	Scriptures to read, pray, & learn
Betrayal, broken trust	Prov. 20:19, Prov. 11:13, Prov. 6:16-19, 1 Chron. 12:17, Mtt. 24:9-11, Mtt. 26:20-22, Jer. 9:5, Jer. 20:9, Prov. 16:28, Prov. 27:6, Deut. 31:6-8, Josh. 1:5, Heb. 13:5, Ps. 12
Bitterness, unforgiveness	2 Cor. 2:4-11, Col. 3:13, 1 Jn. 1:8-10, Mtt. 6:12-15, Mtt. 12:32, Lk. 6:37, Lk. 7:47-50, Ps. 118:5-6
Disappointment, missed expectations	Jer. 29:11, Jer. 17:7-8, Phi. 1:6, Phil. 4:9, Mtt. 6:25-26, Prov. 13:12, Jn. 14:27, Jn 14:1-3, Ps. 10:12-18, Ps. 16:1-5, Ps. 21:2-3
Exhaustion, fatigue, burnout	Gal 6:8-10, Ps. 119:28, Isa. 40:28-31, Heb. 12:5, Mtt. 11:28, Lam. 5:5, Rev. 2:3, Ps. 6
Fear	Ps. 27:1, Ps. 56:3-4 & 11, Ps. 118:6, Lk. 12:4-12, Mtt. 8:26, Mtt. 4:27-30, Mtt. 10:28, Jn. 14:27, Josh. 1:8-9, Joh. 10:8, Neh. 4:4, Ruth 3:11, Ps. 18
Guilt, conviction	Ps. 7:1-5, Ps. 38, Ps. 51, Prov. 21:8, Ps. 69:5-6, Gen. 3:10-13, Jms. 5:16
Isolation, loneliness	Ps. 68:6, Lk. 5:16, Prov. 12:26, Prov. 17:17, Ex. 33:11, Prov. 18:24, 1 Sam. 20:42, Prov. 22:11, Ps. 16:5, Ps. 102:11, Jn. 15:11
Regret, remorse, shame	Ps. 22:5, Ps. 34:5, Ps. 25:2-3, Ps. 44:6-8, Ps. 69:6, Ezra 9:5-15

©Sue Schlesman 2023

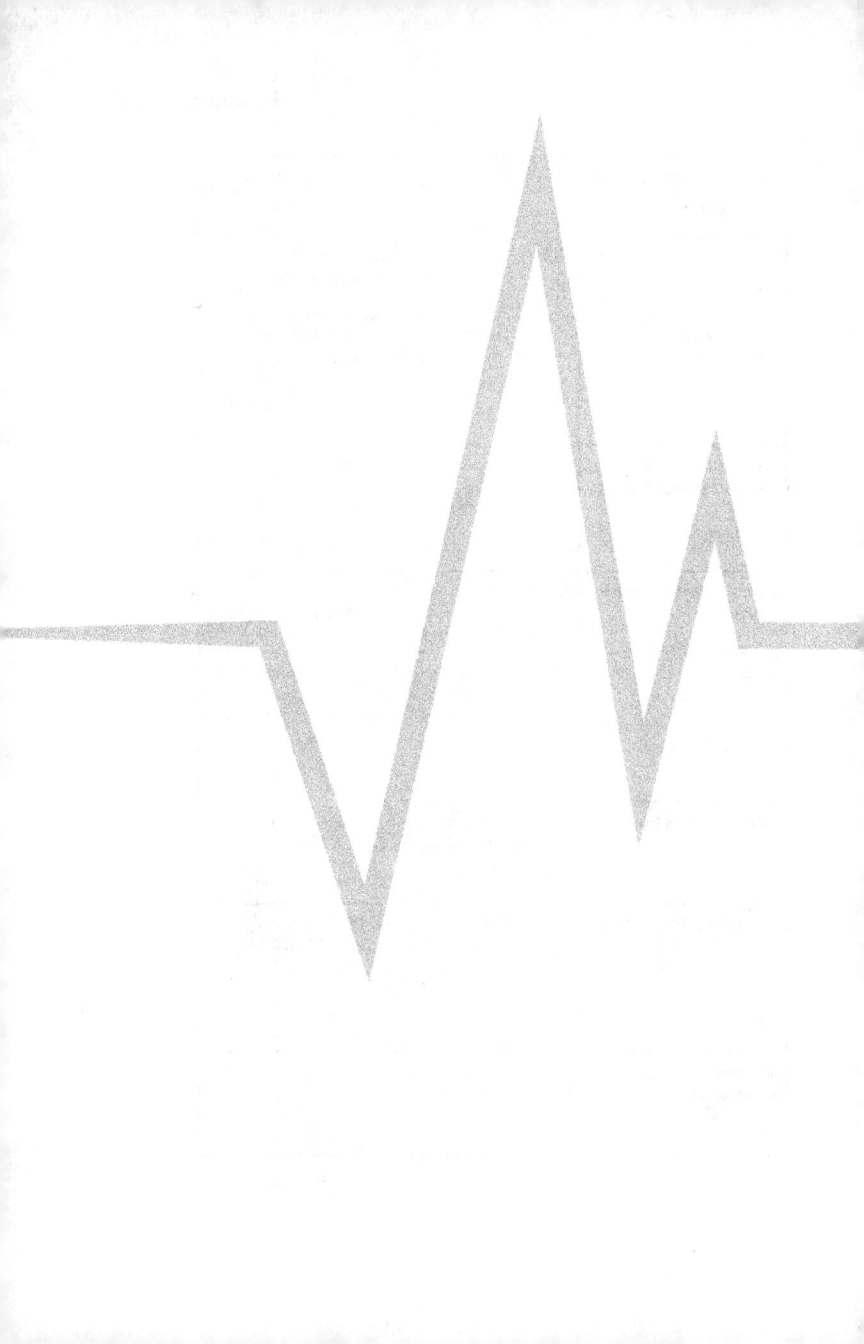

TRACING BEHAVIOR BACK TO BELIEF

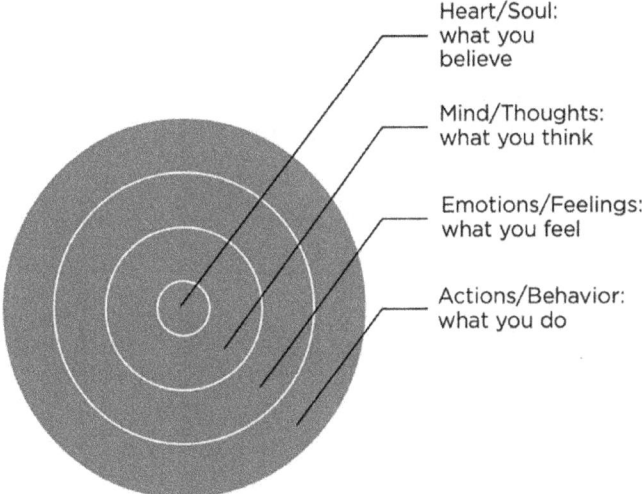

Verse: 2 Corinthians 10:3-5 "For though we live in the world, we do not wage war as the world does. The weapons we fight with are not the weapons of the world. On the contrary, they have divine power to demolish strongholds. We demolish arguments and every pretension that sets itself up against the knowledge of God, and we take captive every thought to make it obedient to Christ."

Discuss the spiritual connection between resilience and truth. What lies do we tell ourselves when we're afraid or upset? How do those lies prevent us from rebounding in faith?

Re-read 2 Corinthians 4:16-18. How do you keep from "wasting away"? What renews you "day by day"? How can you train yourself to trust the process of resilience?

Example 1:
- » ACTIONS: I behave in a passive-aggressive manner when someone provokes me
- » EMOTIONS: I feel anger and defensiveness over their implied criticism
- » MIND: I think I will feel better about myself if I put them down
- » HEART: I believe I deserve their respect and admiration (i.e., I believe my value depends on it)

Example 2:
- » ACTIONS: I avoid telling someone they've hurt or offended me
- » EMOTIONS: I feel afraid, insecure, betrayed, angry, or bitter
- » MIND: I think ignoring this person protects me and punishes them
- » HEART: I believe that I deserve to be loved and appreciated by this person (i.e., my happiness is paramount to me showing this person love)

Example 3:
- » ACTIONS: I monopolize conversations and micro-manage discussions, decisions, and process
- » EMOTIONS: I feel afraid, panicked, or vulnerable in new situations out of my control
- » MIND: I think that everything must be done to my standard because my standard is the best
- » HEART: I believe that God will be more pleased if things are done to my standards (i.e., success depends on my perfection)

Death by *Pastoring*

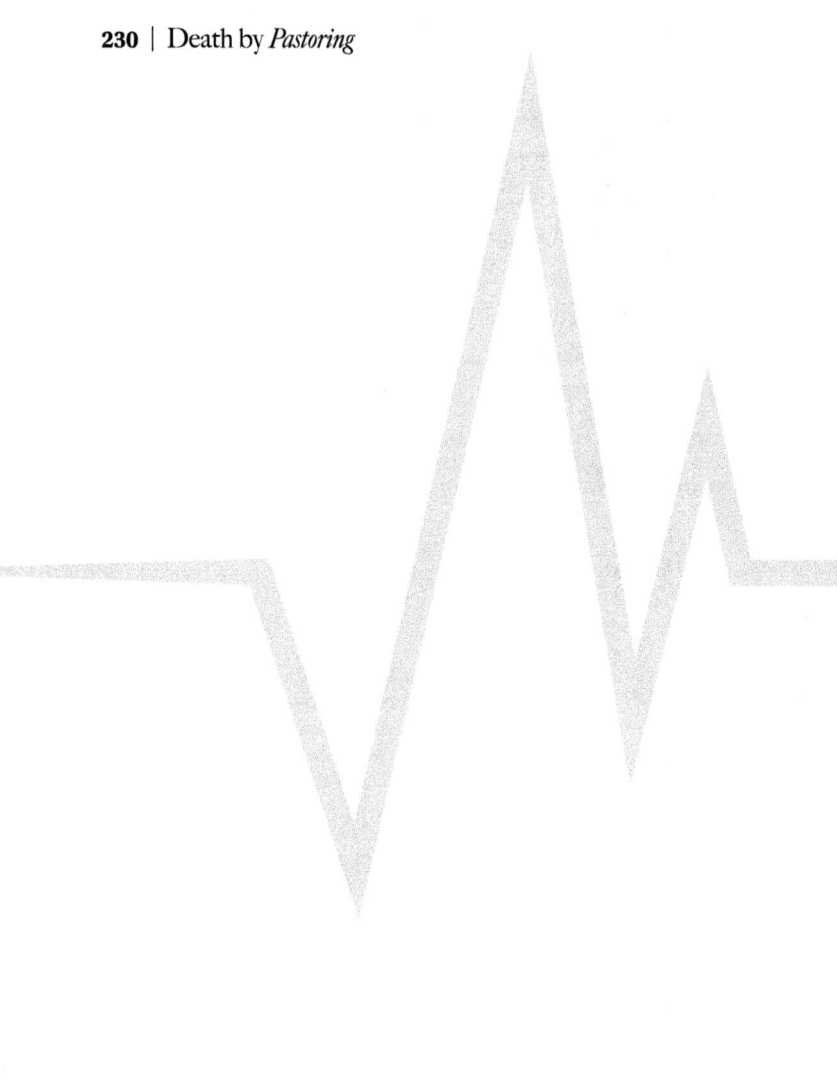

RESILIENCE & AVOIDANCE ASSESSMENT

Directions: Without overthinking it, mark the first answer you believe is true about your natural self. You can check more than one response, but you should answer quickly and trust your gut. There are no wrong answers. I have intentionally omitted responses like "pray," "trust God," "serve God," etc. because these are *learned responses from a Spirit-directed life*. We want to identify our *natural responses and inclinations* because that's what makes us either avoid or adapt to suffering; our natural responses generally inform our behavior. At best, our spiritually directed decisions must fight against our natural responses to pain and discomfort.

1) Which daily decision do you hate the most?
   - ❏ What to wear
   - ❏ What to make for dinner
   - ❏ What to say or not say
   - ❏ What task to do first
   - ❏ Who to give your time to
   - ❏ How to control your emotions
   - ❏ How to approach someone about a problem

2) Before you begin your tasks for the day, what do you usually do first?
   - ❏ Make a list of all the things you need to do
   - ❏ Surf social media
   - ❏ Call or text someone to complain about your work
   - ❏ Get your heart and body in the right framework to work
   - ❏ Set up your workspace
   - ❏ Straighten up your house or office space

3) When you have a long list of tasks to do, what do you do first?
   - ❏ The easiest thing
   - ❏ The most noticeable thing
   - ❏ The worst/hardest thing
   - ❏ Nothing/something that doesn't need to be done

4) Your designated workspace is
   - ❏ Non-existent
   - ❏ Messy
   - ❏ Pretty
   - ❏ Efficient and professional-looking
   - ❏ Organized
   - ❏ Comfortable
   - ❏ Inviting

5) Your mind functions best/you're most productive
    - ❏ In the morning
    - ❏ In the afternoon
    - ❏ In the evening
    - ❏ At night when people are sleeping
    - ❏ In an office space
    - ❏ At a coffee shop
    - ❏ Outside
    - ❏ In a retreat location

6) You do your best work when you're
    - ❏ In a small group
    - ❏ By yourself, with headphones on
    - ❏ With a close friend
    - ❏ In front of an audience
    - ❏ In complete privacy

7) Your downtime/de-stressor time mostly includes
    - ❏ Physical activity or exercise
    - ❏ Watching shows
    - ❏ Surfing social media
    - ❏ Talking to friends
    - ❏ Eating
    - ❏ Reading
    - ❏ Learning/education
    - ❏ Escape: travel, spa, salon, shopping

8) You are most upset by
   - ❑ Criticism or belittling of your performance or accomplishments
   - ❑ Exclusion from a social activity
   - ❑ Being ignored or untouched by a loved one
   - ❑ Forgotten or down-played holidays, birthdays, or celebrations
   - ❑ Isolation
   - ❑ Injustice/tragedy in the world or your personal environment
   - ❑ Critique or suggestion about how you could improve yourself
   - ❑ Not being affirmed or recognized for your accomplishments
   - ❑ Conviction that you have done something wrong
   - ❑ Gossip about you or a loved one
   - ❑ Betrayal of trust by a friend or co-worker

9) The person who usually causes you the most stress is
   - ❑ Your parent
   - ❑ Your sibling
   - ❑ Your friend
   - ❑ Your spouse/significant other
   - ❑ Your in-law
   - ❑ Your boss
   - ❑ Your co-worker
   - ❑ Your neighbor

- ❏ Your ex
- ❏ Your peer group or general church body

10) Your worst fear is
    - ❏ Not being successful
    - ❏ Not being considered successful
    - ❏ Not being happy
    - ❏ Not pursuing my dreams
    - ❏ Not being in control
    - ❏ Being alone
    - ❏ Being unloved
    - ❏ Being hurt
    - ❏ Being in a dangerous situation
    - ❏ Getting sick/being unhealthy
    - ❏ Dying

11) Where do you regularly experience pain and discomfort?
    - ❏ Someone cries or falls apart emotionally in your presence
    - ❏ You feel deep loss or grief
    - ❏ You feel embarrassment or shame about your life
    - ❏ You witness violence or verbal assault among close family or friends
    - ❏ Someone around you is rude, rebellious, or disrespectful to authority
    - ❏ You experience physical pain in your body

- ❏ Someone in your family experiences deep emotional or physical pain
- ❏ You are disappointed or despairing about how something turns out
- ❏ You are disturbed by the choices of a large group of people or culture in general

12) How would you most like to be described?
    - ❏ Inclusive
    - ❏ Hard-working
    - ❏ Generous
    - ❏ Hospitable
    - ❏ Intelligent
    - ❏ Forgiving
    - ❏ Well-liked
    - ❏ Accomplished
    - ❏ Perceptive/wise
    - ❏ Inspiring
    - ❏ Just/fair

13) When I experience difficult circumstances or trials, my natural response is
    - ❏ Isolate myself/shut down
    - ❏ Call friends or family for comfort
    - ❏ Ignore it or refuse to accept it as true
    - ❏ Retaliate, attack, or refute
    - ❏ Figure out how to solve the problem myself

- ❏ Ask someone to help me figure it out
- ❏ Plan or involve someone to help change the circumstance

14) How do you typically handle a situation where someone hurts you deeply?
    - ❏ Lovingly confront them and try to reconcile the relationship
    - ❏ Avoid them and hope your hurt feelings pass
    - ❏ Pray and forgive them without confrontation (but still struggle with your hurt)
    - ❏ Get angry and tell them how much they wronged you
    - ❏ Get angry and rant to someone else about how much they wronged you
    - ❏ Become more cautious or cynical about relationships in the future; have trouble trusting again
    - ❏ Figure out a way to retaliate or punish them or facilitate punishment/retribution for them

EXPLANATION OF AVOIDANCE ASSESSMENT

Directions: Write your response from the self-check in the blanks below. Re-consider the question and the related topic. Highlight any responses that cause you concern.

1) **QUESTION:** Which daily decision do you hate the most?

_____

_____

_____

TOPIC OF QUESTION: Decision-making, priorities, habits

2) **QUESTION:** How do you prepare for your workday?

_____

_____

_____

TOPIC OF QUESTION: Planning, habits

3) **QUESTION:** When you have a long list of tasks to do, what do you do first?

_____

_____

_____

TOPIC OF QUESTION: Priorities, planning, values, mood

Resources | 239

4) **QUESTION:** What is your workspace like?

_____

_____

_____

TOPIC OF QUESTION: Environment, mood, feeling, relationships

5) **QUESTION:** When are you most productive?

_____

_____

_____

TOPIC OF QUESTION: Body check: mind, soul, spirit, emotions

6) **QUESTION:** How do you work best?

_____

_____

_____

TOPIC OF QUESTION: Group and personal relationships

7) **QUESTION:** How do you de-stress?

_____

_____

_____

TOPIC OF QUESTION: Body check: coping skills, personality

8) **QUESTION:** What are you most upset by?

_____

_____

_____

TOPIC OF QUESTION: Emotional triggers, values, personality, shaping influences

9) **QUESTION:** Who causes you the most stress?

_____

_____

_____

TOPIC OF QUESTION: Anxiety, personal relationships, insecurity

10) **QUESTION:** What scares you?

_____

_____

_____

TOPIC OF QUESTION: Shaping influences, emotional triggers

11) **QUESTION:** Where do you regularly experience pain or discomfort?

_____

_____

TOPIC OF QUESTION: Emotional triggers, perspective, adaption

12) **QUESTION:** What do you want to be known for?

TOPIC OF QUESTION: Legacy, values, goals

13) **QUESTION:** How do you naturally respond to suffering?

TOPIC OF QUESTION: Coping mechanisms, emotional awareness, empathy, faith

14) **QUESTION:** How do you handle a situation where someone hurts you deeply?

TOPIC OF QUESTION: Confrontation, personal relationships, shaping influences, wisdom

Do you see any behavior patterns emerging on this chart? Find one place to improve and give it to God. If he's bringing it to your attention, it's because he wants you to let him fix it. But you must take that step of obedience and let him do it. And you must do the work.

FIGHT FEAR ASSESSMENT

DIRECTIONS: On the following pages, highlight or circle your top six fears below. Then consider the categories on the right. Look up the verses pertaining to your biggest fears.

Memorize them.

I'm afraid of being embarrassed or judged.	I'm afraid to share the gospel or my testimony.	I'm afraid of disagreement or confrontation with people; I'm afraid of making enemies.	I'm afraid of trusting people with my emotions and inner feelings.
I'm afraid of trusting other people's decisions if they affect me.	I'm afraid of listening/not controlling a conversation.	I'm afraid to travel outside the U.S.A.	I'm afraid to start new jobs, habits, friends, hobbies, etc.
I'm afraid of losing relationships or disappointing people.	I'm afraid of getting counseling or probing into my heart/mind.	I'm afraid of not doing enough, of never being successful.	I'm afraid of getting old or feeling irrelevant.
I'm afraid of being alone.	I'm afraid of not having enough money.	I'm afraid my kids won't turn out, that they will get sick, or that they will die.	I'm afraid of getting a disease and/or dying.

I'm afraid of conversations with my boss.	I'm afraid of meeting new people.	I'm afraid of rejection.	Psalm 56:11 Psalm 118:6 Isa. 54:4 Heb. 13:6 Psalm 3:6 Psalm 55 Eph. 6:19-20
I'm afraid of the government's control & laws that hinder my freedoms.	I'm afraid of working under or for someone else.	I'm afraid of not being in control.	John 14:27 Josh. 1:9 Josh. 10:25 Psalm 46:1-3
I'm afraid people will find out about my past or present secrets/pain.	I'm afraid to say "no" to opportunities, obligations, and/or people.	I'm afraid of not being worthy.	Isa. 44:21 John 4:17-18 Psalm 34:4 Psalm 139:1116
I'm afraid of natural disasters, car accidents, assault, and/or home invasion.	I'm afraid of inflation, stock market crash, war, world catastrophes.	I'm afraid of the future.	Rev. 2:10 Psalm 27:1 Prov. 3:24 Psalm 23:4-5 Phil. 1:14 1 Peter 3:5-7

©Sue Schlesman 2022

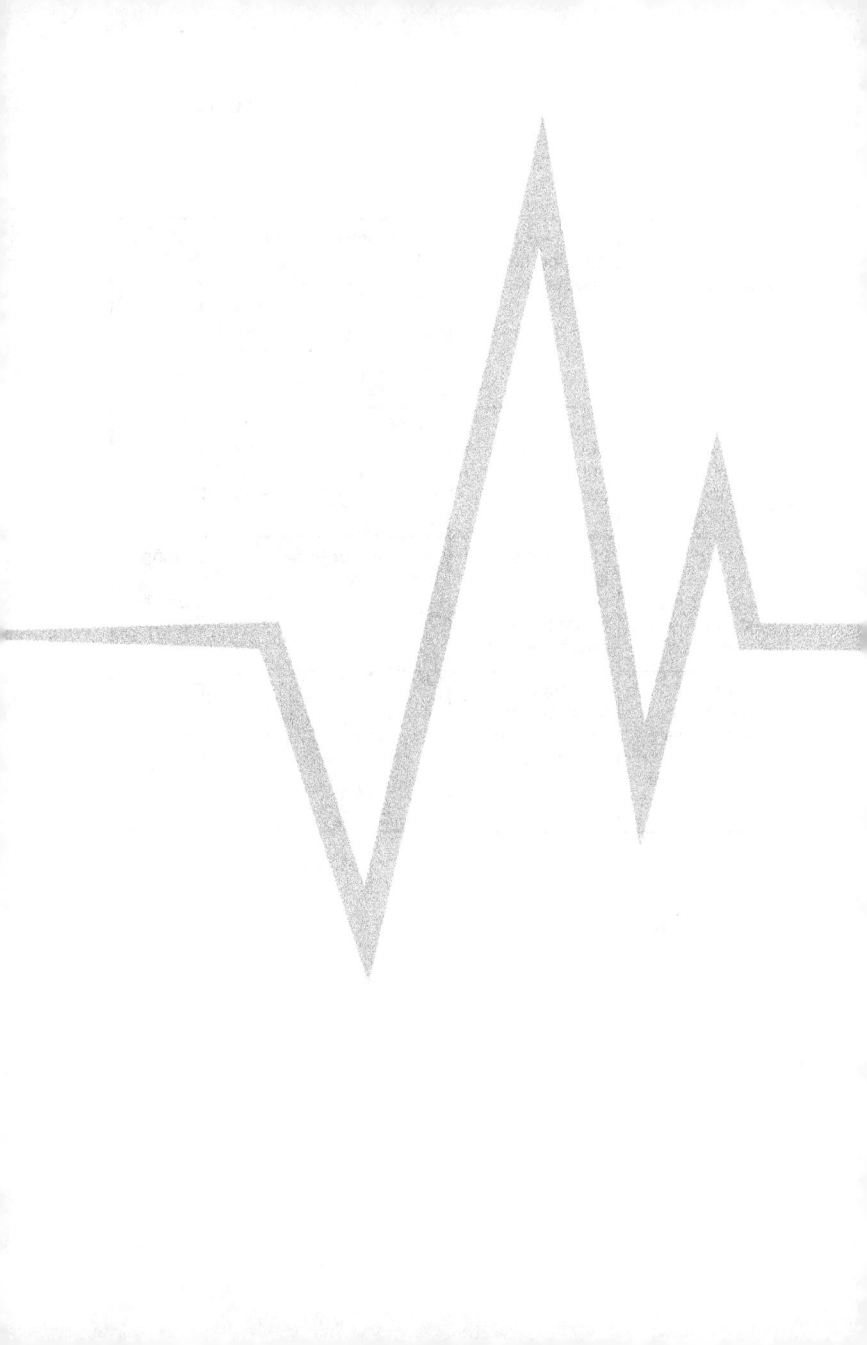

SOURCES

PART 1 —The Silent Killer (The Problem of Pain)
Chapter 1—The Almost-Death of a Pastor (and His Wife)

1. "Pastors Share Top Reasons They've Considered Quitting Ministry in the Past Year," 27 Apr. 2022, Barna Research, Barna.com/research/pastors-quitting-ministry/
2. "38% of Pastors Have Thought About Quitting Full-time Ministry in the Last Year," Barna Research, 16 Nov. 2021, https://www.barna.com/research/pastors-well-being/
3. "Year in Review: Barna's Top 10 Releases," 21 Dec. 2022, Barna Research, Barna.com/research/year-in-review-2022/
4. "Pastors Share Top Reasons They've Considered Quitting Ministry in the Past Year," 27 Apr. 2022, Barna Research, Barna.com/research/pastors-quitting-ministry/
5. Christopher Ash, *Zeal Without Burnout,* The Good Book Company, 1 March 2016.
6. Glenn Packiam, *The Resilient Pastor*, Baker Books, 15 Feb. 2022.

Chapter 2 — The DNA of Stress

1. Bessel Van Der Kolk, M.D., *The Body Keeps the Score: Brain, Mind, and Body in the Healing of Trauma*, Penguin Books, 8 Sept. 2015.

2. "Stress effects on the Body," March 8, 2023, American Psychological Association, https://www.apa.org/topics/stress/body
3. Fred Shaffer and J.P. Ginsberg, National Library of Medicine, "An Overview of Heart Rate Variability Metrics and Norms," https://www.ncbi.nlm.nih.gov/pmc/articles/PMC5624990/
4. Vincent Luppino, PT, DPT, OCS, "How to Use Heart Rate Variability in Your Training," Hospital for Special Surgery, https://www.hss.edu/article_heart-rate-variability.asp
5. "Stress Symptoms," Mayo Clinic, https://www.mayoclinic.org/healthy-lifestyle/stress-management/in-depth/stress-symptoms/art-20050987
6. Matt Henslee, "3 Areas of Stress for a Pastor," Lifeway Research, 8 June 2022, https://research.lifeway.com/2022/06/08/3-areas-of-stress-for-a-pastor/
7. "Pastors Who Want to Quit, Self-care and Soul-care Slip," 15 June 2022, Barna Research, https://www.barna.com/research/spiritual-formation-back-seat

Chapter 3 — What We Didn't Learn in Seminary

1. "Excerpt: What Pastors Wish They'd Been Prepared For," Barna Research, 19 April 2023, https://www.barna.com/research/pastors-better-prepared/
2. "7-Year Trends: Pastors Feel More Loneliness and Less Support."
3. Trevin Wax, "Your Pastor's Wife Probably Feels Lonely," Lifeway Research, *The Gospel Coalition*, Nov. 2, 2020, Thegospelcoalition.org/blogs/Trevin-wax/your-pastors-wife-probably-feels-lonely/
4. Philippians 1:21
5. Carey Neuwhof, "7 Signs It's Time to Leave the Church You're Leading," *CareyNeiuwhof.com*, https://careynieuwhof.com/7-signs-time-to-leave/#:~:text=While%20statistics%20vary%2C%20most%20pastors,they%20never%20bring%20about%20transformation.
6. John Maxwell, "Success Stabilizers lesson," Leadership Cohort, Ready Set Grow, 15 Nov. 2023.

7. *Doulos*, G1401, *Blue Letter Bible*, https://www.blueletterbible.org/lexicon/g1401/niv/mgnt/0-1/

Chapter 4 — The Snare of Expectations

1. Sam Chand, *Leadership Pain*, Thomas Nelson, 2015.
2. Matthew 22:36-37

Chapter 5 — A Bottomless Place

1. Chris Foy, "Are Mental Disorders Increasing Over Time?", World Health Organization, FHE Health, 1 Feb., 2023, fherehab.com/mental-health-disorders-increasing#:~:text=Statistics%20from%20the%20World%20Health,for%20those%20age%2015%2D29.
2. "Mental Health," *The Unstuck Church Podcast* with Tony Morgan, Episode 80, Sept. 30, 2022
3. Marsea Nelson, 29 June 2011, "Ten Interesting Facts About Lions," World Wildlife Fund, https://www.worldwildlife.org/blogs/good-nature-travel/posts/ten-interesting-facts-about-lions#:~:text=A%20lion%20can%20run%20for,4.
4. Sue Schlesman, "How to cope with loss," *Sueschlesman.com*, 9 Aug. 2016, www.sueschlesman.com/how-to-cope-with-loss/
5. Karen Blandino, LCSW, *Stress Test Podcast*, Episode 20, 13 December 2023.
6. Isaiah 61:1-3
7. Sue Schlesman, "Grief sucks," *Sueschlesman.com*, Sueschlesman.com/grief-sucks, 22 August 2016.

PART 2 — A New Way to Work (The Hope for Stress)
Chapter 7 — The Pathway to Peace

1. Matthew 5

Chapter 8 — Leading in a Yoke

1. "Oxen," https://www.lancasterfarming.com/oxen-no-has-beens-when-it-comes-to-hard-pulling/article_b79a5f8f-5d4b-578d-997a-f385095dc7c9.html
2. Philippians 2:1-4 (The Message)
3. "Compassion Fatigue: Signs, Symptoms, and How to Cope," Canadian Medical Association, Dec.8, 2020, www.cma.ca/physician-wellness-hub/content/compassion-fatigue-signs-symptoms-and-how-cope

Chapter 9 — Stewards and Owners

1. *Kairos,* G2540, Ephesians 5:15-16, *Blue Letter Bible,* https://www.blueletterbible.org/lexicon/g2540/niv/mgnt/0-1/
2. Dave Ramsey, "Leading with Stewardship", YouTube, https://www.youtube.com/watch?v=F0E18v5jHc0

PART 3 — A New Way to Rest (The Redemption of Stress)
Chapter 12 — Rest Versus Restoration

1. Šûḇ. Restore, H7725, Psalm 23:3, *Blue Letter Bible,* https://www.blueletterbible.org/lexicon/h7725/niv/wlc/0-1/
2. Ṣeḏeq, H6664, Psalm 23:3, *Blue Letter Bible,* https://www.blueletterbible.org/lexicon/h6664/niv/wlc/0-1

Chapter 13 — New Walk, Same Valley

1. Clinton McCann Jr, "Psalms," *The New Interpreter's Bible Commentary*, Vol. IV, Abingdon Press, 1996, 768.

Chapter 15 — The House of the Lord

1. Scott Wilson, Nuts & Bolts Conference, Potomac District Assembly of God, 3 Dec. 2020.
3. *Tobe,* H2895, Psalms 23:6, *Blue Letter Bible,* https://www.blueletterbible.org/lexicon/h2896/niv/wlc/0-1/
4. *Hesed,* H2617, Psalm 23:6, *Blue Letter Bible,* https://www.blueletterbible.org/lexicon/h2617/niv/wlc/0-1/

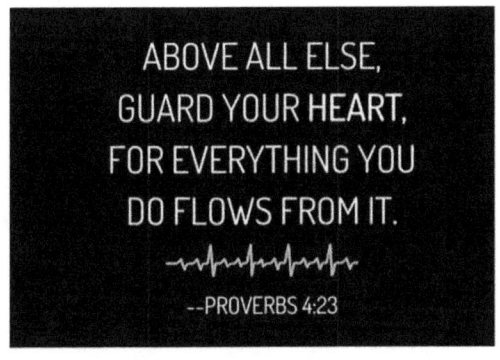

CONTACT INFORMATION:

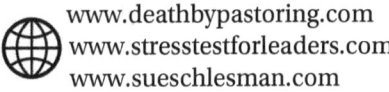
www.deathbypastoring.com
www.stresstestforleaders.com
www.sueschlesman.com

🅕 Stress Test

🅞 @stresstest_podcast

▶ Stress Test Podcast: The Heartbeat of a Healthy Leader

🎙 Stress Test: The Heartbeat of a Healthy Leader

🅢 Stress Test: The Heartbeat of a Healthy Leader

To join our community, text "STRESS" to
this number and follow the prompts to
receive resources, new episodes, etc.:

(833) 204-2158

THE AVAIL PODCAST
HOSTED BY VIRGIL SIERRA

FOLLOW THE LEADER

STAY CONNECTED

 facebook.com/TheArtofAvail   @theartofavail   **AVAIL**

AVAIL+

TRY FOR 30 DAYS *AND RECEIVE*
THE SEQUENCE TO SUCCESS BUNDLE FREE

$79 VALUE

+ BOOK
+ STUDY GUIDE
+ ONLINE COURSE
+ LIVE CLASS
+ MORE

The Art *of* Leadership

This isn't just another leadership collective...this is the next level of networking, resources, and empowerment designed specifically for leaders like you.

Whether you're an innovator in ministry, business, or your community, **AVAIL+** is designed to take you to your next level. Each one of us needs connection. Each one of us needs practical advice. Each one of us needs inspiration. **AVAIL+** is all about equipping you, so that you can turn around and equip those you lead.

THEARTOFLEADERSHIP.COM/CHAND

www.ingramcontent.com/pod-product-compliance
Lightning Source LLC
Chambersburg PA
CBHW070530090426
42735CB00013B/2925